This Book must be returned to
the Library on, or before, the
last date shown below

19 JUN 1961

PUBLISHED WITH THE AID OF A GRANT

FROM

THE AMERICAN COUNCIL OF LEARNED SOCIETIES

INSTITUTE OF FINE ARTS · NEW YORK UNIVERSITY

STATUES ON COINS

OF SOUTHERN ITALY AND SICILY IN

THE CLASSICAL PERIOD

BY

PHYLLIS WILLIAMS LEHMANN

H. BITTNER AND COMPANY · NEW YORK

1946

c

TO THE MEMORY

OF

HARRIET BOYD HAWES

TABLE OF CONTENTS

PREFACE

THE AIM of the present study is two-fold: to propose the thesis that Greek coinage of the classical period includes a certain number of numismatic types which are neither more nor less than faithful reproductions of contemporary statues and to present a method whereby sculptures may be attributed to a given region, in this instance Southern Italy and Sicily, by virtue of a precise relationship to specific coins.

I am particularly indebted to Karl Lehmann for his fruitful suggestion that this problem was worth investigating, and for ideas too numerous to be recorded in the notes. Under his patient and critical direction, I prepared this manuscript as a dissertation for New York University. It stands virtually unchanged.

Without the unique facilities of the American Numismatic Society, I should have been lost, indeed. I am grateful to its staff for extending the privileges of the Society to me and especially to Sidney P. Noe and Agnes Baldwin Brett for many valuable suggestions. It is a pleasure to recall the interest and advice of the late E. T. Newell and to thank Gisela M. A. Richter for having given my manuscript the benefit of her criticism. I should like to acknowledge the assistance of Margarete Bieber, Marjorie Milne, and Mary H. Swindler, and to offer my special thanks to Walter W. S. Cook and Rensselaer W. Lee.

Finally, I should like to repeat my gratitude to the Alumnae Association of Wellesley College for having made this study possible by awarding me the Horton-Hallowell Fellowship for 1939–1940. Thanks to the Archaeological Research Fund of New York University, I was enabled to supplement my studies by visiting several important South Italian and Sicilian collections in August 1939 on my return from the Fund's expedition to Samothrace.

Some of the results of this study were presented at the forty-third general meeting of the Archaeological Institute of America in December 1941, a brief summary of which appeared in the *American Journal of Archaeology*, XLVI, 1942, p. 119.

P. W. L.

ABBREVIATIONS

A.A.	*Archäologischer Anzeiger. Beiblatt zum Jahrbuch des deutschen archäologischen Instituts.*
A.J.A.	*American Journal of Archaeology.*
A.M.	*Mitteilungen des deutschen archäologischen Instituts, Athenische Abteilung.*
ARNDT-BRUCKMANN	H. Brunn, P. Arndt, F. Bruckmann, *Griechische und römische Porträts,* Munich, 1891 —
BdA	*Bollettino d'arte.*
BR.-BR.	H. Brunn, F. Bruckmann, *Denkmäler griechischer und römischer Sculptur,* Munich, 1897 —
BUL.COM.	*Bullettino della Commissione archeologica comunale di Roma.*
EINZELAUFNAHMEN	*Photographische Einzelaufnahmen antiker Skulpturen,* Munich, 1893 —
FURTWÄNGLER, *Masterpieces*	Adolf Furtwängler, *Masterpieces of Greek Sculpture,* ed. by Eugénie Sellers, New York, 1895.
G.A.	*Gazette archéologique.*
G.B.A.	*Gazette des Beaux-Arts.*
GROSE	S. W. Grose, *Catalogue of the McClean Collection of Greek Coins,* Cambridge, 1, 1923.
HEAD, *Guide*	Barclay V. Head, *A Guide to the Principal Coins of the Greeks,* London, 1932.
HEAD, *H.N.*	Barclay V. Head, *Historia Numorum,* Oxford, 1911.
JAHRBUCH	*Jahrbuch des deutschen archäologischen Instituts.*
J.H.S.	*Journal of Hellenic Studies.*
J.O.A.I.	*Jahreshefte des österreichischen archäologischen Institutes in Wien.*
N.S.	*Notizie degli scavi.*
NUM. CHR.	*Numismatic Chronicle.*
R.A.	*Revue archéologique.*
RE	Pauly-Wissova-Kroll, *Real-Encyclopädie der classischen Altertumswissenschaft,* Stuttgart, 1894 —
REINACH, *Répertoire*	Salomon Reinach, *Répertoire de la statuaire grecque et romaine,* Paris, 1897 —
R.M.	*Mitteilungen des deutschen archäologischen Instituts, Römische Abteilung.*
R.N.	*Revue numismatique.*
ROSCHER	W. H. Roscher, *Ausführliches Lexikon der griechischen und römischen Mythologie,* Leipzig, 1884 —
ZfN	*Zeitschrift für Numismatik.*

A   B   C

Fig. 1. London, British Museum: A. Reverse of Tetradrachm of Naxos. B. Reverse of Didrachm of Herakleia. C. Reverse of Stater of Metapontum

INTRODUCTION
A Numismatic Approach to Sculpture

The scantiness of literary references to Magna Graecia and Sicily and the attendant lack of specific information about works of art once visible in its cities and sanctuaries have forced those investigating the plastic style of this region to pay more than usual attention to its minor arts. Hence it is that the rarely beautiful coins issued by the cities of Southern Italy and Sicily have served as the basis of more than one illuminating study of regional style.[1] Like the local terracottas, they have been interpreted as dependable reflections of the general stylistic development of their time, and looked upon as welcome fixed points about which to group stylistically similar statues and statuettes.[2] Convincing as these analogies have been in many cases, in general they have not led to the further assumption that the coin types and sculptures of this region may be iconographically related as well.[3] Nor is this surprising.

For although it has long been recognized that the study of coins affords an invaluable approach to many a debated problem of the history of sculpture,[4] and it is universally agreed that a quantity of late Hellenistic and Roman coins reproduces known statues,[5] the opinion still prevails that in the heyday of the classical period the die-cutter was an artist to whom "exact and servile imitation of things"[6] did not occur; that "as long as Greek art was alive, an exact or slavish copy of a statue or relief was all but unknown."[7] The

1. The investigations of Bernard Ashmole (*Late Archaic and Early Classical Greek Sculpture in Sicily and South Italy*, from the *Proceedings of the British Academy*, xx, London, 1934) and G. E. Rizzo (*Saggi preliminari su l'arte della moneta nella Sicilia greca*, Rome, 1938; *Intermezzo*, Rome, 1939) are especially noteworthy.
2. A method best exemplified by Ashmole in the above-cited work. See, too, his "Relation Between Coins and Sculpture," *Transactions of the International Numismatic Congress*, 1936, London, 1938, pp. 17–22. The fact that this approach to the problem was entirely neglected or overlooked by Ulf Jantzen in his *Bronzewerkstätten in Grossgriechenland und Sizilien*, Berlin, 1937, is astonishing.

3. Sporadic instances of such connections between specific coin types and sculptures have been made and will be referred to whenever they touch upon types discussed in this study.
4. A method recommended by Raoul-Rochette, "Conjectures archéologiques sur le groupe antique dont faisait partie le torse du Belvédère," *Mémoires de l'Institut Royal de France. Académie des Inscriptions et Belles Lettres*, xv, 1842, pp. 251 ff. Note, for example, the use of numismatic evidence in such a case as that of Agorakritos' statue of Nemesis for Rhamnous (J. P. Six, "Aphrodité-Némésis," *Num. Chr.*, Ser. iii, vol. ii, 1882, pp. 89 ff.; Gisela M. A. Richter, *The Sculpture and Sculptors of the Greeks*, New York, 1930, pp. 239–240; Charles Picard, *Manuel d'archéologie grecque*, Paris, ii, 1939, p. 537 and note 2).
5. The instances in which this has been proved are too numerous to be cited. See, for example, the basic article of F. Imhoof-Blumer and Percy Gardner, *A Numismatic Commentary on Pausanias*, reprinted from *J. H. S.*, 1885, 1886, 1887; Percy Gardner, "Copies of Statues on Coins," *Corolla Numismatica*, London, 1906, pp. 104 ff., etc. S. Mirone, "Copies de statues sur les monnaies antiques de la Sicile," *R. N.*, ser. iv, vol. xxiii, 1920, pp. 3–5, lists an extensive bibliography for these cases.
6. Percy Gardner, *The Types of Greek Coins*, Cambridge, 1883, p. 68.
7. *Ibid.*, p. 19.

1

doctrine of the essential artistic independence of archaic and classical coin types, of the creative freedom of the die-cutter has been enunciated again and again, with ever-increasing emphasis and precision,[8] despite the protests of certain dissenters.[9] Unfortunately, the most articulate and active member of this opposition confused the issue by offering inadequate arguments in support of a basically just contention.[10]

Indeed, it can scarcely be denied that such a coin type as the well-known Apollo stater of Metapontum (Fig. 1C) immediately creates the impression of a statue or, more precisely, of the reproduction of a statue.[11] The exceptionally plastic rendering of the figure and the fact that it is by no means particularly well adapted to its circular field are the two factors primarily responsible for this effect. However, it is largely because of its striking relationship to a passage in Herodotus that this type is generally agreed to represent a lost statue. Other equally plastic looking types lacking such a literary connection have not fared so well. And their number is considerable.

It is obvious that many coin types are purely numismatic inventions designed to fill a circular space. The famous Naxian satyr[12] (Fig. 1A) exemplifies this group. Every detail of the decoratively disposed parts of the body from the curving legs to the balanced patterns of arms, legs and torso, from curving beard, tail and kantharos to the dis-

8. The foremost modern exponent of this theory was Kurt Regling (*Die antike Münze als Kunstwerk*, Berlin, 1924, pp. 89 ff.) whose opinion was shared by such other writers on the subject as A. Sambon ("L'art monétaire antique en Grande-Grèce et en Sicile," *L'Acropole*, II, 1927, p. 90), F. Matz ("Ein Zeuskopf in Villa Borghese," *Jahrbuch*, XLVI, 1931, p. 26) and Charles Seltman (*Greek Coins*, London, 1933, p. 107). G. F. Hill (*Select Greek Coins*, Paris and Brussels, 1927, p. 23) gives a somewhat modified acquiescence to this position. For a final discussion of Regling's views see "Die Münzen als Hilfsmittel der archäologischen Forschung," *Handbuch der Archäologie*, ed. Walter Otto, Munich, 1939, pp. 134–144.

It would be fruitless to discuss Regling's general philosophy of art or to itemize all the details of his argument with which I disagree. His basic thesis in itself is contradicted by the results of the present investigation. However, it may be well to point out that Regling's contention (p. 136) that "Die älteren Bronzestatuetten kopieren z. B. nur höchst selten die frühere oder gleichzeitige Grossplastik" collapses if only on the evidence of the numerous small bronze replicas and variants discussed in the limited field of the present study. So, too, Regling did not recognize that the original die of a coin type reproducing a contemporary statue is naturally more faithful to the stylistic details of that work than dies made thirty or forty years later by craftsmen who, while retaining the numismatic type in all its essentials, modify it in order to make it more up-to-date. To him, such modifications necessitated either the supposition that the statues themselves were replaced every decade or two in correspondence with the contemporary fashion reflected in later dies—an idea which neither Regling nor anyone else would accept—or the assumption that the copies of a statue would invariably remain fixed, an alternative unquestionably contradicted by the history of the copying of statues. The pitfalls of misapprehension into which the cult of the "freedom of the die-cutter" leads are nowhere more evident than here. It is not that the first copyist was less free than others so much as that the sculptor and the first copyist were working in contemporary styles while the later copyist faced an entirely different situation. As Jean Babelon recognized in his review of *Die antike Münze als Kunstwerk* (*Arethuse*, III, 1926, p. xv), Regling's own case was weakened by the number and types of exceptions to his rule that he felt compelled to cite. If the psychology of the Hellenistic or Roman die-cutter who reproduced a statue was so utterly foreign to that of his classical predecessor, how is one to account for the point of view of the unorthodox creators of these exceptions and of the magistrates' symbols occurring on early coins which everyone agrees reproduce statues? It is hardly adequate to eliminate the latter with the statement that "Dass in diesen minutiös kleinen Zeichen Werke der Grossplastik wiederholt sind, ist um so weniger auffallend, als sie wie die oben besprochenen wechselnden Haupttypen wohl vom jeweiligen Münzbeamten, nicht unmittelbar von der Staatsregierung vorgeschrieben waren" ("Die Münzen als Hilfsmittel," *op. cit.*, p. 138).

9. Especially Babelon, *loc. cit.*, and à propos of certain types discussed by Ernest Babelon, *Traité des monnaies grecques et romaines*, Paris, 1907. See, too, P. Lederer, "Die Staterprägung der Stadt Nagidos," *Z. f. N.*, XLI, 1931, p, 171, note 1; B. Pace, *Arte e*

civiltà della Sicilia antica, Milan, 1938, II, pp. 63 ff. and the older work of A. Joubin, *La sculpture grecque*, Paris, 1901, pp. 253, 274–275. George MacDonald, *Coin Types*, Glasgow, 1905, p. 97, clearly leaned in this direction, as does Ashmole, "Relation Between Coins and Sculpture," p. 20.

10. Mirone, *loc. cit.*, and its supplement, *R. N.*, ser. IV, vol. XXV, 1922, pp. 1 ff. and successive articles: "Copies de statues sur les monnaies de la Grande-Grèce," *R. N.*, ser. IV, vol. XXVII, 1924, pp. 1–28; 1925, pp. 1–16; "L'influence de la sculpture et de la peinture sur les types monétaires de la Grande-Grèce et de Sicile au Ve siècle avant J. C.," *Arethuse*, II, 1925, pp. 69 ff., III, 1926, pp. 11 ff., pp. 68 ff. Three methodical weaknesses of the author's argumentation require special attention. Mirone accepts numerous coin types as reproductions of statues solely on the grounds that there is evidence of the existence of a temple or cult of a given divinity in a particular city, in which case he assumes that there must have been a cult statue and that it probably appears as the coin type—all of which may or may not be true but, in any case, is pure theory. Secondly, exception must be taken to his use of literary sources: Agrigentum presented a statue of the river god Akragas to Delphi; a head of the god appears on its coinage; therefore, the coin type is a copy of the statue! ("Copies de statues . . . de la Sicile," p. 12). Finally, although he proposes ("Copies de statues . . . de la Grande-Grèce," p. 1) to enumerate the statues mentioned by ancient authors which can be identified with similar coin types, and to add comparisons with statuary replicas wherever they exist, by not really making a thorough investigation of sculpture he not only overlooked the monumental evidence for the two Metapontum Apollo types discussed in the present study which he, too, suggested as copies of statues but, ironically enough, he never proposed as possible copies of statues the several types discussed in these pages for which there is unquestionable monumental evidence.

11. Hill, *op. cit.*, pl. XXXIX, 4; here text Fig. 1C. For a more complete discussion of the type see pp. 33 ff.

12. *Ibid.*, pl. XXXVIII, 1; here text Fig. 1A.

tribution of the letters of the inscription reflects the die-cutter's desire to create an appropriate design for a flat, circular space. On the other hand, such an effective numismatic type as Herakles wrestling with the Nemean lion on the coinage of Herakleia in Lucania (Fig. 1B)[13] also occurs in sculpture. Nevertheless, even if it were possible to prove that this type originated in Herakleia, the fact that it is used on the contemporary coinage of several other cities in various parts of the Greek world precludes the possibility of associating a statuary group of unknown provenance with it, since it would be impossible to determine to which of the several regions the group should be attributed, or whether one of the coin types was a purely numismatic adaptation of another.[14]

However, if such a coin type were unique, its value would increase tremendously. For if a statue of unknown provenance is iconographically and stylistically identical with a coin type, and that numismatic type is unique, struck at a specific time by one, and only one, city, it is logical to assume that statue and coin type alike depend upon a common archetype. Such a coin type not only constitutes a reproduction of a given statue; by virtue of its own unquestionable provenance, it affords the means of attributing closely related sculptures to a given region, hence, of enlarging the number of works which may reasonably be considered products of that region.

In applying this method to the problem of South Italian and Sicilian sculpture, I have limited my investigation to the period extending from 480 to 323 B.C. The first step was to select from the coinage of this time and region all those coin types which, from a purely visual standpoint, give the impression of reproducing full-length statues.[15] The next step was to examine whatever Greek and Roman sculptures were available in published form, from small bronzes and terracottas to monumental sculptures, to see whether any figures iconographically related to those numismatic types could be found. This comparative examination of the numismatic and plastic evidence allowed the following conclusions: that there are at present ten coin types of Magna Graecia and Sicily between 480 and 323 B.C. for which there is monumental evidence, and that these coin types reproduce famous lost statues and constitute focal points about which numerous statues and statuettes may be grouped. These ten coin types are discussed in the following pages. The additional types, of equally statuesque appearance, for which no such monumental evidence is as yet available have been eliminated from the present discussion. Some of them may well reproduce statues but at the moment it is not possible to prove that they do.[16]

It cannot be too emphatically repeated that each of the numismatic types presented here is iconographically unique, occurring in no other part of the ancient world. This may be said to be the cardinal principle of the present approach, without which the entire method would collapse. Furthermore, the procedure outlined here must be strictly observed if the results are to have any validity. Lack of precision in comparisons of supposedly similar coins and statues—the relating of bearded to unbearded types, of figures standing on the right leg to those standing on the left, of types characterized by slightly different attributes —can do and has done more to discredit the possibilities of this method than the most adamant theoretical opposition.[17]

Before turning to the ten South Italian and Sicilian types about which the discussion will revolve, it may be well to illustrate the method employed in the succeeding pages by glancing at two coins issued by Herakleia in Lucania early in the third century B.C. Since it is generally agreed that Hellenistic coins sometimes reproduce statues, the choice of examples in this period should afford an opportunity to clarify the method used throughout this study without rais-

13. *Ibid.*, pl. XLVII, 5; here text Fig. 1B.
14. It is unnecessary to discuss all the possible interrelationships between numismatics and painting, or such coin types as are loosely related to broad stylistic and iconographic trends in contemporary monumental art. Innumerable varieties of all these interrelations exist. However, they lie outside the scope of the present discussion.
15. This investigation did not consider representations of heads or animals. Nor did it include statues used in a secondary, subordinate position as symbols, as, for example, on the well-known Corinthian staters (A. Blanchet, "Representations de statues sur des statères de Corinthe," *R. N.*, ser. IV, vol. XI, 1907, pp. 317–323) or, in the region under discussion, the Palladion on a Tarentine coin (Mirone, "Copies de statues . . . de la Grande Grèce," pp. 3 ff.).

16. See appendix.
17. Thus the Herakles type of Herakleia discussed on pp. 53 ff. differs from the similar earlier fourth-century stater type of Issos in Cilicia (F. Imhoof-Blumer, *Monnaies grecques*, Amsterdam, 1883, pl. F21) in that the latter has a left instead of a right *Standbein*, and a resulting rhythmic reversal indicative of a different statuary type.

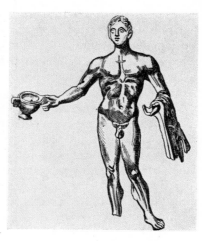

FIG. 2. Former Colson Collection, Noyon: Bronze Statuette of Herakles

FIG. 3. Paris, Bibliothèque Nationale: Bronze Statuette of Herakles Found near Naples

FIG. 1. Cambridge, Fitzwilliam Museum: Reverse of Stater of Herakleia

FIG. 4. Berlin, Antiquarium: Bronze Statuette of Herakles from the Abruzzi

FIG. 5. Cambridge, Fitzwilliam Museum: Reverse of Didrachm of Herakleia

FIG. 7. Naples, Museo Nazionale: Marble Puteal

FIG. 6. Rome, Museo Nazionale: Marble Statue of Herakles

PLATE I

ing the controversial issue of chronology. These examples will suffice to illustrate the method of iconographic and stylistic comparison to be followed as well as the range of monuments to be considered, a range including bronze and marble statues and statuettes, classical originals and neoclassical reflections. If this method proves acceptable in the present instances and similar evidence can be presented for coins falling within the period from 480 to 323 B.C., its validity should be established.

About 295 B.C., Herakleia issued staters with Herakles, god of prosperity and dispenser of abundance, as the reverse type.[18] The hero-god stands almost facing (Pl. 1, Fig. 1), his head turned to his right, as he pours a libation over a flaming altar from a jug in his extended right hand. In his left arm, over which a lion's skin is flung, he carries a cornucopia.[19] The familiar club leans against his right leg. Given the marked plasticity of the figure and the arrangement of the attributes, the impression that the coin type reproduces a cult image or votive statue is immediate. The existence of precisely this iconographic type in bronze statuettes provides ample support for such an hypothesis.

A bronze statuette (Pl. 1, Fig. 2) once in the Pourtalès and later in the Colson collection[20] presents a beardless, youthful Herakles facing slightly toward his right, with his weight placed on his right leg, and his left resting lightly to the back and side. Over his left arm he carries a lion's skin,

while in his hand he holds a cornucopia. His extended right hand grasps the vertical, rectangular fragment of a missing attribute. His short locks are bound by the peaked fillet popular in Southern Italy.[21] Iconographically, statuette and coin type are identical. The fact that the cornucopia carried by the statuette is smaller than that on the coin is of no importance. Seemingly, the cornucopia on the coin is filled with fruit, whereas the statuette carries phalli. In either case, the meaning is clear; the contents of both cornucopias are equally symbolic of fertility, of that natural fecundity in all aspects of life which the god has power to grant.[22] The similarity of coin type and statuette indicates the proper restoration for the missing attribute of the latter's right hand. Obviously, it held a jug, and the existing vertical fragment is the original handle.[23]

Stylistically, too, the figures have in common a slender, wiry build and an emphatically hip-shot stance. The line-engraved illustration does not permit a more detailed stylistic analysis; to judge by it, the statuette is of Roman execution.[24]

The Bibliothèque Nationale in Paris owns a

ΕΦΣΩΔ

18. ϜΗΡΑΚΛΕΙΩΝ to right downward;   ΑΜ·Σ to left, below right arm. Obverse: head of Athena to right wearing crested Athenian helmet. ΝΙ behind neck. Grose, pp. 113–114, pl. XXIX, No. 17 [Pl. 1, Fig. 1]. Specifically dated by Sir Arthur Evans, "A Recent Find of Magna-Graecian Coins of Metapontum, Tarentum, and Heraclea," *Num. Chr.*, ser. IV, vol. XVIII, 1918, pp. 153 ff., where it is pointed out that the full names of officials first appear on Tarentine coinage in the period 302–281 B.C. This fact, plus the correspondence between the obverse Athena type and a Metapontine coin issued by Agathokles, enabled Evans to suggest the unusually precise date quoted above. I am indebted to Mr. Sidney P. Noe for this reference.

19. Not an attribute of Herakles until after the archaic period (cf. A. Furtwängler's article: *Herakles* in Roscher, I², col. 2157). Whether or not it refers specifically to Herakles' conquest of Acheloos or to Amaltheia, the cornucopia symbolizes the fertility of nature. Hence it is generally filled with fruit and plants and, occasionally, with phalli (cf. the article *Hercules* by F. Dürrbach in Daremberg and Saglio, *Dictionnaire des antiquités grecques et romaines*, Paris, 1900, III, 1, 78 ff.).

20. Ht: 22 cm. Provenance unknown. A. Colson, "Hercule Phallophore," *G. A.*, III, 1877, pp. 168–171, pl. XXVI; Reinach, *Répertoire*, II¹, p. 218, no. 4. The statuette appears as fig. 1 in the text of *Denkmäler*, No. 770, where it is quoted in connection with a related but by no means identical type of Herakles.

21. Furtwängler, *op. cit.*, col. 2176. Colson, *op. cit.*, misinterpreted this peak as the crescent of the moon and considered it indicative of the nocturnal setting of Herakles' amorous adventures with the daughters of Thestios. In a later article, "Hercule Phallophore," *Annales du Musée Guimet*, IV, 1882, pp. 39 ff., Colson quoted MM. de Witte and Lenormant as considering the statue a syncretistic, pantheistic creation in which the crescent symbolizes Diana. Such an explanation is manifestly erroneous. This detail is not visible on the coin.

22. As Furtwängler remarked, *loc. cit.*—Colson's explanation, *G. A.*, *loc. cit.*, of the phalli as a direct reference to Herakles' exploits among the daughters of Thestios is a quaint but uncalled for interpretation. For it is not the hero or any of his deeds that are celebrated here, but a god of fertility to whom homage is paid.

23. Colson, *ibid.*, restored a club. However, the angle of the arm and the height at which it is held forbid such a restoration. Either the club would dangle in the air or it would have to rest on a large rock. The amount of space left between the fingers, their position, and the rectangular section of the fragment preclude that explanation. The figure is so clearly a Herakles that MM. de Witte and Lenormant's suggestion, *ibid.*, a caduceus, may be ignored save as an indication of the width of the original attribute. R. P. Hartwig, *Herakles mit dem Füllhorn*, Leipzig, 1883, p. 59, proposed a bow. Quite apart from theoretical objections to this suggestion, the analogy between the Colson statuette and the Herakleia stater as well as the evidence provided by a similar statuette in the Bibliothèque Nationale now to be discussed excludes any thought of a bow.

24. Colson, *ibid.*, quoted Feuardent as considering the figure Gallo-Roman and made in Lyons at the time of Caesar or Augustus. Colson, himself, considered it more Greek than Roman, and suggested Provence as a possible provenance (*Annales*, pp. 42–43). Furtwängler, *loc. cit.*, described the statuette as "grossgriechisch." This may be the basis of Jean Bayet's reference to it (*Les origines de l'Hercule romain*, Paris, 1926, p. 412, note 9)

figure of identical type.[25] It, too, is a small bronze statuette of mediocre Roman workmanship (Pl. 1, Fig. 3). Again, a youthful, beardless Herakles stands on his right leg, his left behind and to the side. The long-waisted, long-legged figure, the somewhat raised left shoulder, and the ranginess of the chest are reminiscent of the coin type, while the short curly locks outlining the face specifically recall the Colson bronze. However, in this instance, it is the attribute of the left arm that is missing. The properly placed lion's skin is preserved, but the hand is empty. Nevertheless, the position of the fingers, the thumb and index fingers being extended, the others grouped together and cupped, attests the original presence of a cornucopia,[26] as a comparison with the Colson Herakles proves. The extended right hand holds a kantharos. This slight transformation of the original type may reflect a fusion of it with the popular *Hercules bibax*. It is of particular interest that this statuette was found in the environs of Naples.[27]

Thus the statuesque appearance of the Herakleia coin type is vindicated. It surely reproduces a contemporary statue of Herakles which also survives in two bronze statuettes, one of undoubted South Italian provenance. The fact that these small copies are of considerably later workmanship suggests the likelihood that the lost archetype existed as late as the first century B.C.[28]

Probably the best indication of the style of this

lost statue is provided by an approximately contemporary variant of the type now in Berlin (Pl. 1, Fig. 4).[29] This charming bronze statuette shows Herakles carrying a cornucopia in his left hand over which a lion's skin hangs, and standing in a position parallel to that of the coin type save for two details: his head is turned toward his left, and his right arm hangs down at his side and clasps a broken unidentifiable object.[30] Otherwise, the easy boyish grace of the figure, the contour of the body and legs, the anatomical schematization of the torso, and the rendering of the knees are exactly like the representation on the coin. In addition, the rather small ears and the short curls around the brow are reminiscent of both the Colson and the Bibliothèque Nationale statuettes. Indeed, the stylistic similarity of the Berlin figure and the coin type is so striking as to allow only one explanation: the statuette must be a contemporary variant of the lost archetype. The fact that the Berlin statuette comes from the Abruzzi gives added weight to this suggestion.

Thus the lost statue reproduced on this Herakleia stater about 295 B.C. must have been made about the end of the fourth century B.C. Iconographically, it survived in two bronze statuettes, one in the Colson collection, one in the Bibliothèque Nationale; stylistically, it may be reconstructed as identical with the contemporary variant in Berlin.[31]

Having seen an example of a numismatic-plas-

as a bronze "de l'Italie Méridionale." If he based his statement on any facts in regard to the provenance, he does not cite them.
25. No. 561. Ht: 14 cm. Green patina. Right foot and attribute of left arm missing. Restored with a club by E. Babelon and J. A. Blanchet, *Catalogue des bronzes antiques de la Bibliothèque Nationale*, Paris, 1895, p. 234. Formerly in the Caylus Collection, and mistakenly illustrated in reverse in A. C. P. Caylus, *Recueil d'antiquités*, Paris, 1762, V, p. 118, pl. XLVI, 3, 4. Note, however, that Reinach, *Répertoire*, II¹, p. 221, Nos. 2, 7, reproduced both the Caylus and Bibliothèque Nationale versions, and quoted the Caylus reference for both without correcting the mistake or realizing that they illustrate the same statuette.
26. Not a club, for when Herakles holds his club in a comparable position, he invariably grasps its top with all his fingers which are then seen in an almost vertical, up-side-down position.
27. Caylus, *loc. cit.*
28. Furtwängler, *op. cit.*, col. 2176 mentioned a terracotta statuette, apparently of this type, in the museum at Taranto. It appears to be unpublished.

The occurrence of small reproductions of a monumental image is entirely understandable insofar as such statuettes were votive gifts and, as such, reflections of an iconic type. When such miniature figures performed a different function, for example, as mirror handles their adaptation to a given type must be regarded as evidence of purely formal inspiration.

29. No. 6476, Antiquarium. The only details mentioned in the *Führer durch das Antiquarium*, Berlin and Leipzig, 1924, I, p. 40, pl. LIV are that it is from the Abruzzi and has the smooth, light green patina of Italian bronzes. It is described as of careful, fourth-century workmanship. However, it may well belong to the very end of the century. Reproduced by Reinach, *Répertoire*, VI, p. 52, No. 4, and mentioned by Hartwig, *op. cit.*, p. 59.
30. Very likely the handle of a vessel. The contents of the cornucopia are not clearly discernible in the photograph.
31. It is interesting to note that Furtwängler, *loc. cit.*, considered the Herakleia coin and the Colson and Berlin statuettes as evidence of the popularity of the iconographic type of Herakles with a cornucopia in Southern Italy.

From 281 to 272 B.C., Herakleia issued two similar staters (cf. Grose, pl. XXIX, Nos. 18, 21). However, the fact that on one the hero is shown more frontally, that he is of a more mature build, that his right hand leans on a club, and that he wears a baldric which he appears to grasp with his left hand indicates that the figure represents a different statuary type. On the other, he holds a club in place of his cornucopia. Without further evidence, it is difficult to define the precise relationship of these types to the earlier didrachm and/or its archetype. They may simply be numismatic variations of the earlier didrachm. Note, too, that *ca.* 89 B.C., the bronze coinage of Uxentum bore a type close to the

tic relationship marked by the presence of a striking and relatively unusual iconographic element insofar as Herakles representations are concerned, let us turn to one characterized by a highly individual representation of a standard attribute. It is hardly necessary to repeat that in each case the stylistic evidence is as important as the iconographic.

The reverse of a didrachm issued by Herakleia from about 281 to 272 B.C. (Pl. I, Fig. 5),[32] shows a nude youthful Herakles standing with his weight on his left leg, his right placed obliquely forward and to the side, and leaning jauntily on his club with his bent right arm, his left being enveloped by the lion's skin. Again, the exceptional plasticity of the rendering of this lithe, athletic figure gives the impression that the coin type reproduces a statue. In this instance, the correctness of such an assumption is borne out by the irregular, rocky support for the club, a detail represented in an unpictorial manner foreign to a purely numismatic concept and inexplicable save as the literal reflection of an actual plastic support.

Furthermore, the dependence of this numismatic type on a statuary prototype is assured by the existence of an exactly analogous statue, the Ludovisi Herakles[33] (Pl. I, Fig. 6). A comparison of Figs. 5 and 6 indicates not only the typological identity of coin and statue, including such details as the slightly forward, oblique position of the right leg, the precise spot on the thigh against which the knobby club is held, as well as its rocky support, but also the exact stylistic similarity of the two. The same vigorous forms, the same separation of the shoulders from the chest, of the ribs from the abdomen, the same emphatic fold over the groin and wide V of the pelvis, the same full thighs, the same silhouette characterize both figures. The ungainly support over which the lion's skin of the Ludovisi Herakles falls is the familiar addition of the Roman copyist[34] translating a bronze original into marble. But the unusual motif of the lion's skin wrapped around the left forearm, veiling the hand, while the head and paws dangle, is common to both representations. The one detail in which coin and statue differ— the direction in which Herakles' head is turned— is undoubtedly the result of a numismatic variation caused by the addition on the majority of dies of a small figure of Nike flying toward the hero from his left. Faced with the problem of including this accessory figure in the available space, the die-cutter could hardly have placed it otherwise. The resulting necessity of turning Herakles' head toward Nike goes without saying, and may be dismissed as a minor modification which in no way

latter, *ibid.*, p. 108, Nos. 800–803; *Real Museo Borbonico*, Naples, IV, 1827, pl. XV, No. 7. The suggestion made by Hartwig, *op. cit.*, p. 68, that the Uxentum type was derived from that of Herakleia is probably right, as was his idea that statuary types lay behind them. Note, too, the considerably later bronze coin of Assorus (Grose, p. 249, No. 2142, pl. LXVIII, 12) on which the local river god Chrysas presents a figure similar to the Herakleia type. By varying the attributes, notably by replacing the hero's lion's skin with a chlamys, and the rendering of the slim, youthful figure, the type has been adapted to serve as a river god. Whether this particular application of the type reflects the influence of sculpture or numismatics cannot be determined.

A. Furtwängler, *Beschreibung der Vasensammlung im Antiquarium*, Berlin, 1885, II, No. 3879 described a fragmentary plate stamped with a relief of a bearded Herakles otherwise identical with the coin type. He considered it either a free rendering of the coin or an unknown variety. The absence of the bearded Herakles on the coins of Herakleia makes the former explanation more likely. Rudolf Pagenstecher, *Die Calenische Reliefkeramik (Jahrbuch, Ergänzungshefte,* VIII), Berlin, 1909, pp. 15, 21, thought that this fragment and others like it were probably manufactured in Rome where the majority of examples have been found, although H. Heydemann, *Mitteilungen aus den Antikensammlungen in Ober- und Mittelitalien (Drittes Hallisches Winckelmannsprogramm)*, Halle, 1879, p. 27 and Dressel, "La suppellettile dell' antichissima necropoli esquilina," *Annali*, LII, 1880, p. 293, note 1, had considered them South Italian. For the most recent discussion of this third-century ware see Inez Scott Ryberg, *An Archaeological Record of Rome from the Seventh to the Second Century B.C. (Studies and Documents,* XIII¹), University of Pennsylvania Press, 1940, pp. 123 ff., where it is also considered of Roman workmanship. The stamps and coins discussed on p. 124, par. 1 reflect different statuary types.

32. Obverse: Head of Athena to left wearing helmet; reverse:

φιλο in field to left; Herakles as described, generally crowned by Nike flying from his left. Grose, No. 861, pl. XXX, 4 [Pl. I, Fig. 5].

33. Formerly in the Villa Ludovisi (Theodor Schreiber, *Die antiken Bildwerke der Villa Ludovisi in Rom*, Leipzig, 1880, p. 71, No. 45), now in the Museo Nazionale in Rome (R. Paribeni, *Le Terme di Diocleziano e il Museo Nazionale Romano*, Rome, 1932, No. 169 [8573]). Ht: 1.47 m. Greek marble. Restorations: heel and ankle of left foot; piece of tree with part of base bordering on it; upper half of club, little finger and thumb of right hand. Right upper arm patched. Toes and upper part of lion's skin smoothed off. Repeatedly broken. Head re-set, but ancient, and belonging. Nose restored; lower lip mended; ears smoothed. On front edge of unprofiled base, modern inscription: NEMIO· Mentioned by F. G. Welcker, *Alte Denkmäler*, Göttingen, 1864, V, p. 81, No. 4 and G. Cultrera, "Una statua di Ercole," *Memorie delle R. Accademia dei Lincei, Classe di scienze morali, storiche e filologiche*, Rome, ser. V, vol. XIV, fasc. III, 1910, p. 182 and fig. 1. Also reproduced by Reinach, *Répertoire,* II¹, p. 209, No. 1 and V, p. 80, No. 9. Fig. 6: Photo Chauffourier, No. 1738.

34. The heavy Roman execution of the figure was indicated by Schreiber, *loc. cit.*, and Paribeni, *loc. cit.*

7

affects the fundamental similarity of the two figures.

There can be only one explanation of the extraordinary analogy between the Herakleia didrachm and the Ludovisi Herakles: both statue and coin must reflect a common archetype, and that archetype must have been a bronze statue made shortly after 300 B.C.[35] which stood in Herakleia and was of sufficient local importance to be reproduced on the city's coinage and to be copied afterward.

The Ludovisi Herakles is not the only later reflection of the lost archetype. It appears again, in what may be called a direct quotation, on a neoclassical marble puteal in the Museo Nazionale in Naples[36] (Pl. 1, Fig. 7). Among the seven divinities forming a frieze around the puteal is a youthful Herakles so obviously identical with the Ludovisi Herakles and the Herakleia didrachm as to require no further comment.[37] These interrelationships permit two major conclusions: first, that

the statuesque-looking didrachm type, far from being a purely numismatic creation, does, indeed, reproduce a lost statue; and second, that the Ludovisi Herakles is a faithful copy of a South Italian statue and, as such, constitutes just as legitimate an example of the sculpture of that region as any fragment of architectural relief.

Having illustrated the correct application of the method by means of two examples which fall slightly beyond the chronological limits of this study and may, therefore, serve as a bridge between the later Hellenistic and Roman periods for which the truth of this method is recognized and the earlier classical period for which it is not generally accepted, let us proceed to a consideration of ten well-known coin types of Magna Graecia and Sicily. All ten fall within the period from 480 to 323 B.C. Each is iconographically unique, having occurred in no other region of the ancient world. The validity of this attempt to enlarge the stock of assured South Italian and Sicilian sculptures is emphasized by the fact that only one of the ten, the Metapontine stater, reproduces a statue for which there is documentary evidence as well— a graphic indication of how insufficient an approach to the problem the available literary sources afford. The immediate aim of the present study is to establish these ten numismatic types as dependable reproductions of lost local sculptures in order that they may afford the means of attributing hitherto unassociated statues and statuettes to the production of this region. In this fashion, one more avenue of approach to the complex problem of South Italian and Sicilian sculpture may be opened up.

35. A date compatible with Welcker's and Schreiber's classification of the statue, *loc. cit.*, as Lysippan, and with Paribeni's description of it, *loc. cit.*, as a Roman copy possibly deriving from a work of Lysippos' circle. See, too, B. Graef, "Herakles des Skopas und Verwandtes," *R. M.*, IV, 1889, p. 214, note 2.

36. No. 289. From the Farnese Collection. Inv. Sangiorgio 532. Ht: 1.04 m.; dia.: 0.86 m. Seated Zeus, with Ares, Apollo, Asklepios, Dionysos, Herakles, Hermes (A. Ruesch, *Guida illustrata del Museo Nazionale di Napoli*, Naples, n.d., p. 94. Present illustration, Fig. 7 taken from fig. 24 of the English edition of the guide). Also published in the *Real Museo Borbonico*, Naples, I, 1824, pl. XLIV, pp. 5 ff., and Gerhard-Panofka, *Neapels antike Bildwerke*, Stuttgart and Tübingen, 1828, p. 78, No. 257.

37. Wilhelm Schick, "Zwei römische Kolossalstatuen und die hellenistische Kunst Syriens," *Neue Jahrbücher für das klassische Altertum*, XXXIII, 1914, pp. 18 ff., considered the Ludovisi Herakles a variant of a lost statue known in two other replicas: the colossal gilded Herakles in the Palazzo dei Conservatori (Galleria superiore II, 5. H. Stuart Jones, *The Sculptures of the Palazzo dei Conservatori*, Oxford, 1926, pp. 282 ff.) and a bronze statuette from Byblos in the British Museum (H. B. Walters, *Catalogue of the Bronzes, Greek, Roman, and Etruscan, in the British Museum*, London, 1899, No. 827). He attempted to prove that this hypothetical lost statue was a cult image of Melquarth made for Tyre in the second century B.C. and explained the totally different motif of the Ludovisi Herakles' left arm as the invention of a copyist translating a bronze original into marble. However marked certain similarities between the Ludovisi Herakles and the Conservatori colossus, the fact remains that they constitute two different statuary types, one characterized by the lion's skin wrapped about the left forearm, the other by the apples of the Hesperides held in the extended left hand. The existence of an identical iconographic type on the coinage of Herakleia proves that the motif of the Herakles Ludovisi cannot be explained simply as the awkward result of a translation from bronze to marble. The independent existence of such an iconographic type is attested not only by the didrachm but also by the Naples

puteal, neither of which was discussed by Schick. To be sure, the Ludovisi and Conservatori statues are close enough to each other stylistically to suggest that the Conservatori Herakles may stem from the prototype of the Ludovisi, and constitute a derivation from and re-creation of the earlier Ludovisi type. The Ludovisi Herakles, itself, may stand in a similar relationship to what must be an earlier statuary type reflected on the coinage of Herakleia and illustrated by Grose, pl. XXIX, 16. Schick's theory, including his highly questionable use of an idealizing head of Melquarth on the coinage of Tyre to reconstruct a specific, full-length figure, was accepted by Jones, *loc. cit.*

Cf. Louis Couve, "Fouilles à Délos," *Bulletin de correspondance hellénique*, XIX, 1895, p. 477 and fig. 4, for a statuette that seems to be a derivation from and transformation of the Herakles Ludovisi in which the skin has been replaced by a mantle.

A bronze coin of Germe ad Caicum of the Antonine period (Grose, III, pl. CCCII, 18) appears to be a late echo of the Herakleia type discussed above.

RIVER GODS

I

SOMETIME BETWEEN 466 and 422 B.C., Leontini issued litrae bearing a youthful divinity, probably the river god Lissos, as the reverse type.[1] The young god approaches an altar and stands on his left leg, his right to the front, as he holds a patera in his extended right hand, a laurel branch in his left (Pl. II, Fig. 1). The angularity of the tall, spare figure, the awkwardness of his stance give him a particularly individual appearance. This same quality characterizes a group of bronze sculptures so closely related to the coin type both iconographically and stylistically as to suggest that it is an unusually faithful copy of a local statue.

Foremost among them is the youth from Castelvetrano[2] (Pl. II, Figs. 2–3). Even a glance at Figs. 1 and 3 suffices to reveal the remarkable similarity of the two. Not only does the bronze statue stand in precisely the same position, with the heel of his right foot in line with the toes of the left, but his very coiffure is repeated on the coin. The single detail in which the figures differ slightly—the angle of the left forearm—is obviously the result of the die-cutter's clarification of a motive to render it more visible. Still more striking is the stylistic analogy of coin and statue. The same jerky rhythm, the same angularity of the slightly bent head and forward leg, the same long waist and pronounced buttocks, even the same schematization of the torso, and profile of the head, shoulders, and legs characterize both figures. There can be little doubt that either the Castelvetrano youth and the Leontini litra reflect a common archetype, or one was directly dependent upon the other, or the statue reproduced on the coin was inspired by the Castelvetrano youth. In any case, the missing attributes of the statue are surely the branch and patera, as the position of the hands in itself has always indicated.[3]

It is not surprising that the Castelvetrano youth, the only bronze statue of sizeable dimensions ever found in Sicily, should have been the subject of considerable discussion. Nor is it remarkable that like many a work of South Italian provenance it has been considered primarily "Doric"[4] or, more specifically, Aeginetan or Sicy-

1. Obv: ꟿEON Head of lion to right, jaws open; border of dots. Rev: as described; corn grain in right field. Wt: 79. Grose, p. 276, pl. LXXVII, No. 6 [Pl. II, Fig. 1]. Generally accepted as representing the river god Lissos (cf. Grose, *ibid.*, and Jean Babelon, *Catalogue de la collection de Luynes*, Paris, 1924, I, No. 1002), but called the river Terias by S. Mirone ("Les divinités fluviales représentées sur les monnaies antiques de la Sicile," *R. N.*, ser. IV, vol. XXI, 1917–1918, p. 18). Hill calls the figure Apollo because of an example in the Ward Collection (in John Ward, *Greek Coins and Their Parent Cities*, London, 1902, p. 30, pl. IV, No. 197) in which he carries both the laurel branch and a lyre in his left hand. Since the coin is otherwise identical with the normal examples, it is more reasonable to interpret it as a numismatic variant, especially given the uncharacteristic feature of two attributes in one hand. The common occurrence of Apollo on the coinage of Leontini may have stimulated this variant as certain parallel functions of the river gods and Apollo (see p. 19 and note 29) would have facilitated their interchange. The persistence of river god types on Sicilian coinage is so marked, as is the analogy between the Leontini litra and the Selinus-Pandosia types discussed in the following pages, that there can be little question that the litra figure is a local river god. Inasmuch as the Lissos and Terias are both rivers of Leontini, and it seems impossible to establish to which of the two gods the coin alludes, the usual interpretation of the figure as the Lissos, a river running below the west slope of the city, has been retained throughout the present discussion.

For references to river gods in general, see the following section.

2. Ht: 84.7 cm. Of bronze 3–7 mm. thick. Hands, left foot, and missing forepart of right foot made separately, cast solid, and soldered on. Left arm and right foot repaired in antiquity. Iris and pupils originally inserted in different material.

Found in 1882, allegedly near Selinus (cf. note 13), broken into six pieces and incrusted with earth; throat, lips badly corroded. Left hand not recovered till 1891. After many years restored by D'Amico of the Syracuse Museum under the supervision of Orsi. For a full account of the technique and restoration of the statue see Pirro Marconi, "Restauro della statua bronzea d'arte greca detta 'L'Efebo di Selinunte,'" *Bollettino d'arte*, VIII, 1928–1929, p. 231; restoration also indicated by E. Boehringer in *A. A.*, 1929, col. 152, figs. 54–56. Major publications: F. Hauser in *Einzelaufnahmen*, Nos. 569–572 and Marconi, *L'Efebo di Selinunte (Opera d'arte*, fasc. I), Rome, 1929.

3. Marconi, *L'Efebo di Selinunte*, p. 6, and Hauser, *loc. cit.*

4. B. Pace, *Arti ed artisti della Sicilia antica*, Rome, 1917 (*Memorie della R. Accademia dei Lincei, Classe di scienze morali, storiche e filologiche*, ser. V, vol. XV, fasc. VI), p. 523. However, in *Arte e civiltà della Sicilia antica*, II, p. 56 Pace described the statue as local Sicilian work with Doric and Attic elements.

FIGS. 2–3. Castelvetrano Museum: Bronze Statue Found near Selinus

FIG. 4. Modena, Reale Galleria e Museo Estense: Bronze Statuette

FIG. 1. Cambridge, Fitzwilliam Museum: Reverse of Litra of Leontini

FIG. 5. Bronze Mirror Handle from Locri Epizephyrii

FIG. 6. Paris, Bibliothèque Nationale: Bronze Statuette

FIG. 7. Bronze Statuette from Norcia

PLATE II

onian[5] in style or, because of its resemblance to Selinuntine art and its obvious sharing of certain details with the Kritian youth,[6] as evidence of Attic influence on Sicily in the late archaic period.[7] Whatever its stylistic antecedents may have been,[8] the Castelvetrano statue is a provincial work through and through, as has long been recognized.[9] Hence that uncouth naïveté, that tense, ill-mastered vitality which are at once his charm and his imperfection. The abrupt movement, the exaggerated forms, the disjointed quality characteristic of the figure are the antithesis of the harmonious, organic beauty of contemporary Attic art. These very qualities undoubtedly account for the date of about 500 originally assigned to the figure, just as that provincialism is compatible with the later, much more convincing date of about 460 B.C.[10]

The typological and stylistic unity of the Leontini coin and the Castelvetrano youth prove that the latter, too, is a similar divinity, and even suggest the possibility that it is the very statue reproduced on the coin. It is curious, indeed, that in former discussions of this statue its connection with the Leontini litra has been entirely overlooked. Undoubtedly, the near-Selinuntine provenance of the bronze was a strong factor in the widely accepted suggestion that because of its similarity to the related coin type of Selinus,[11] it is to be interpreted as the river god Selinus.[12] Such an interpretation is, of course, out of the question given the reversal of stance in the Selinuntine coin and the Castelvetrano statue, quite apart from any other considerations. Nevertheless, in stating that "in der Statue eines der wichtigsten Götterbilder der Stadt vorliegt, das man als παράσημον τῆς πόλεως auf die Münzen setzte," Hauser was on the right track. Applied to Leontini, his dictum is perfectly acceptable. Indeed, given the exceptional similarity between the Castelvetrano statue and the Leontini litra, it is tempting to consider it the original image of the divinity which once stood in Leontini and was reproduced on the city's coinage. On the other hand, if the statue really stood in Selinus originally, it may have been a workshop copy of the Leontini figure or vice versa. Yet, the strange story of the discovery of the statue[13] by no means guarantees its alleged Selinuntine provenance. Thus its identity with the river god of the coin seems more than likely.

Four statuettes made in the course of the following decade 460–450 present marked analogies

5. G. Perrot and C. Chipiez, *Histoire de l'art dans l'antiquité*, VIII, Paris, 1903, p. 501.

6. Humfry Payne and G. M. Young, *The Archaic Marble Sculptures from the Akropolis*, London, n.d., pls. CIX–CXII, No. 698. That such a type as the Kritian youth lies in the background of the Castelvetrano boy is apparent in general terms and in a detail like the coiffure. This does not alter the fact that the latter is obviously an independent local work, whatever may have been the influences under which the artist's style was formed. Some such consideration certainly led Walter Amelung, "Archaischer Jünglingskopf in Hannover," *Jahrbuch*, XXXV, 1920, p. 55, note 1, to call the Castelvetrano boy a provincialization of the type of the Akropolis youth.

7. A. Furtwängler, *Meisterwerke der griechischen Plastik*, Leipzig-Berlin, 1893, p. 76, note 3; H. Lechat, *La sculpture attique avant Phidias*, Paris, 1904, pp. 375, 455 ff.; G. Fougères, *Sélinonte*, Paris, 1910, p. 291, note 1.

8. See note 6.

9. G. E. Rizzo, "Di una statua fittile di Inessa," *Atti della Reale Accademia di archeologia, lettere e belle arti*, Napoli, XXIII, 1905, part II, p. 188; A. della Seta, *Italia antica*, Bergamo, 1928, pp. 141–142; Ashmole, *Late Archaic and Early Classical Greek Sculpture in Sicily and South Italy*, p. 26; V. H. Poulsen, "Der strenge Stil," *Acta Archaeologica*, VIII, 1937, p. 104, and especially Marconi, *L'Efebo di Selinunte*, p. 11 and "La scoltura e la plastica nella Sicilia antica," *Historia*, IV, 1930, p. 665.

10. Marconi, *L'Efebo di Selinunte*, p. 10; implied in Ashmole, *loc. cit.*

11. Discussed on p. 15 and in note 40 of the following section on the Hypsas didrachm.

12. Hauser, *op. cit.* Quoted by Perrot and Chipiez, *op. cit.*, pp. 494 ff., Fougères, *loc. cit.*, Pace, *Arti ed artisti*, p. 523, *Arte e civiltà*, p. 58, and Marconi, *L'Efebo di Selinunte*, p. 12, note 23, the latter preferring not to take a final stand on the matter of interpretation. Noting that the Castelvetrano boy has no horns, Hauser went so far as to suggest that they might have been separately cast and added to the head. Cf. W. Schwabacher, "Die Tetradrachmenprägung von Selinunt," *Mitteilungen der bayerischen numismatischen Gesellschaft*, XLIII, 1925, p. 77.

13. It was supposedly found in a tomb or terracotta box, that is, enclosed within terracotta slabs, a fact which is interpreted as indicating that the statue must have been carried off in antiquity (probably in a moment of danger), buried, and for some reason abandoned. It is clear from the original accounts that the statue was illegally excavated. Under the circumstances, the information accompanying it, that it was found 100 m. east of a certain house where a Selinuntine necropolis existed, is not to be taken too seriously. Marconi admitted that the exact provenance of the statue could not be stated. The story has the ring of an illegal excavation made in the hope of a sale which was found out, the statue being handed over to the authorities and accompanied by a tale, primarily designed to shield someone, according to which the fragments were found in a tomb "nel territorio di Selinunte." Under the circumstances, it is even possible that the statue was spirited away from Leontini, the necropolis of which was being excavated in those very years. For details of the find see Hauser, *loc. cit.*, and Marconi, "Restauro della statua bronzea . . ," *loc. cit.*

to the Leontini litra and the Castelvetrano statue. Earliest and closest to these works is a bronze statuette in Modena[14] (Pl. II, Fig. 4). Compared with the Castelvetrano statue, it will be seen to reflect the same provincialism and, in the proportions and modelling of the entire torso and V-shaped pelvis, in the silhouette of the left arm and the legs, in the large features and the shape of the face, in eyes, nose, and mouth, it is strictly analogous. However, typologically, it differs in several respects—in the greater inclination of the head and its slightly varied coiffure, in the presence of pubic hair, and in stance, for, in an attempt to soften the angularity of the figure, the right foot has not been placed so far forward. Thus, the Modena bronze represents a slight advance over the archetype and, echoing it, should nevertheless be considered a first variant.

Contemporary with the Modena figure and close to it in modified stance is a bronze mirror handle from Locri Epizephyrii[15] (Pl. II, Fig. 5). The erect carriage of the head and the position of the arms, which have been drawn closer to the body, are results of the adaptation of the type to its function as a handle. Interestingly enough, the excavators remarked the typological analogy between this statuette and the Leontini litra. The shape and line of its shoulders and torso are extremely close to the coin.

The next stage in the development of the Lissos type appears in a statuette in the Bibliothèque Nationale in Paris[16] (Pl. II, Fig. 6). Here the right foot has been drawn still farther back, and this modification, along with the heavier, fleshier forms of the torso, carries the type forward to a new harmony and balance. A glance at Plate II,

Figs. 3 and 4, recalls the basis upon which this progress was predicated—a typological similarity apparent even in the coiffure,[17] in the line of the pectoral muscles, the indentation of the waist, the bulging fold over the groin, and in the thoroughly South Italian face. The creator of this statuette had undoubtedly been subjected to another, possibly Attic, influence; nonetheless, his work is so fundamentally related to the Lissos type as to constitute a variant of it made about 450 B.C.[18] This same stage is reflected in still another bronze statuette from the necropolis of Norcia[19] (Pl. II, Fig. 7).

Finally, it is instructive to glance at two applications of the Lissos type outside the immediate region. For the well-known Sciarra bronze, now in Copenhagen,[20] belongs to this group typologically (Fig. 2). Yet in style it is utterly different. Once considered an original work closely related to the Kritian youth,[21] the Sciarra youth is now generally accepted as of local Italian workmanship and as closest of all to the Castelvetrano statue.[22]

14. Reale Galleria e Museo Estense. Ht: 21.5 cm. Bright green patina. Dated by Arndt (Einzelaufnahmen, No. 1956–57) in the second quarter of the fifth century and interpreted as Apollo holding a patera in his right hand, a bow and arrow in his left. Given its analogy to the Castelvetrano statue and the similarity of their left hands, it is legitimate to discard this interpretation. The statuette is described by Langlotz, op. cit., p. 37 as an "italisch-griechische Bronze"; by Poulsen, op. cit., p. 104, as "grossgriechisch" and dating about 460 B.C. It is also reproduced in Reinach, Répertoire, V, p. 330, No. 1.

15. Found in tomb 865 covered with four tiles. Ht. of handle: 18.5 cm. Omphalos phiale soldered onto right hand. N. S., XXXIX, 1913, supplement, p. 39, fig. 49.

16. No. 928. Ht: 17.5 cm. Deep green patina, oxidized on arms and legs. From the De Luynes Collection. Babelon et Blanchet, Catalogue de bronzes antiques de la Bibliothèque Nationale, p. 409.

17. Best seen in the profile view on pl. XCIX of Ernst Langlotz, Frühgriechische Bildhauerschulen, Nuremberg, 1927.

18. Langlotz, op. cit., p. 164, and Winifred Lamb, Greek and Roman Bronzes, London, 1929, p. 155, call the piece Attic and date it a decade or so earlier. As a modernized provincial work, the later date is more likely.

19. N. S., III, 1878, p. 22, pl. I, fig. 10. Judging by the enthusiastic comments in this report, the statuette is very inadequately illustrated.

It is also possible that the figure in Rouen reproduced by Reinach, Répertoire, III, p. 164, No. 4 may belong to this group. Without a better illustration, however, one cannot say.

20. Ny-Carlsberg Glyptothek, No. 28, inventory 2235. Ht: 1.10 m. Dark green, reddish patina. Lacks left arm and inset eyes and teeth. Feet from ankles down, right hand and one third of forearm, entire upper head, bronze restorations of the seventeenth century. Stone base restored. Surface worked over here and there. On left hip, ancient hole, later enlarged, for attachment of attribute. Walls 5–6 mm. thick; bolts on breast and back. Brows, lips, nipples of pure copper. Found on the Janiculum before the mid-seventeenth century and passed into possession of the Barberini family. Thence into the Sciarra collection and finally to Copenhagen. For a lengthy bibliography see F. Poulsen in Br.-Br., Nos. 743–44.

21. A. Furtwängler, "Eine argivische Bronze," Fünfzigstes Programm zum Winckelmannsfeste, Berlin, 1890, p. 151, in opposition to F. Studniczka's Peloponnesian verdict ("Archaische Bronzestatue des Fürsten Sciarra," R. M., II, 1887, pp. 90 ff.). Later, Furtwängler changed his mind, and considered the Sciarra statue Italian ("Neue Denkmäler antiker Kunst," Sitzungsberichte der k. B. Akademie der Wissenschaften zu München, 1897, II, p. 112, note 2 and Kleine Schriften von Adolf Furtwängler, Munich, 1913, II, p. 440).

22. F. Poulsen, Br.-Br., loc. cit., repeating and elaborating Furtwängler's later opinion; and V. H. Poulsen, "Der strenge Stil,"

However, looked at in the light of the Lissos group, it has a rude bulkiness in the torso, a weakening of vigor in the legs, and a stylization of the face reminiscent of neither Greek nor South Italian works; rather, they suggest an Etruscan origin for the piece. Indeed, the Sciarra bronze seems to be a contemporary Etruscan version of the Lissos type.[23]

Last of all comes a bronze youth from Antikythera[24] (Fig. 3), iconographically a close relative of the group, stylistically a thoroughly Greek and slightly later application of the type. All the abruptness, the exaggeration and lack of polish

inherent in the original type have vanished; in their place is a well-bred grace, a clear, harmonious organization of the body that is utterly unprovincial.

Whether the Castelvetrano statue be accepted as the very archetype of the Leontini litra, a statue set up in the city about 460 B.C. and immediately reproduced on its coinage, or as a contemporary copy of that archetype, there can be little question that the litra is a faithful rendering of a Leontinine statue of the same period. And whether the series of bronze statuettes dependent upon this archetype be regarded as conscious, if modified, replicas of it or as less intentional continuations of the type, the importance of that type and its indigenous character cannot be denied.[25] It is more than sufficient to ensure a South Italian attribution for the Castelvetrano statue and the Modena, Locri, Bibliothèque Nationale, and Norcia statuettes.[26]

p. 104, who dated the statue about 460 and said: "Wahrscheinlich ist sie eine italische Arbeit, unter grossgriechischer Beeinflussung entstanden." Picard (*Manuel d'archéologie grecque*, II¹, p. 108, note*1) considered it of "style italiote imitant Sicyone."

23. Studniczka and F. Poulsen, Br.-Br., *loc. cit.*, related it to Greek victor statues.

[As this manuscript goes to press, the publication of P. J. Riis, *Tyrrhenika*, Copenhagen, 1941, issued during the war, has come to my hands. I am glad to note that the author of this book on Etruscan sculpture also considers the Sciarra bronze to be an Etruscan work (cf. pp. 29–30) and that he remarks upon its South Italian affiliations (p. 165).]

24. Ht: 53.5 cm. Eyes, nipples, lips, teeth originally inserted. Toes of right foot, upper surface of left foot, tip of nose, missing. Oldest of the pieces from the Antikythera find. Interpreted as holding a patera in right hand, bow and arrow in left and, therefore, Apollo, by J. N. Svoronos, *Das Athener Nationalmuseum*, Athens, 1908, I, No. 18, p. 41, pl. VIII, 2. V. Staïs, *Marbres et bronzes du Musée National*, Athens, 1907, No. 13397, pp. 299 ff. considered the statuette a small replica of a fifth- or early fourth-century statue. S. Papaspyridi, *Guide du Musée National d'Athènes*, Athens, 1927, No. 13397, p. 220 called it a Roman copy of a Polykleitan work.

25. Cf. note 46 of the following Selinus-Pandosia discussion and remark again that with the exception of the Modena and Bibliothèque Nationale statuettes, the same characteristic lack of pubic hair is found in these figures, too.

26. A similar litra type occurs on the coinage of Stiela. According to Evans ("Contributions to Sicilian Numismatics. II," *Num. Chr.*, ser. III, vol. XVI, 1896, p. 125 f.) and Head (*H. N.*, p. 171), this type appeared around 450 B.C. However, Mirone ("Stiela, Topografia e numismatica," *Z. f. N.*, XXXVIII, 1928, pp. 41 ff.) dated the coin in the preceding decade and interpreted it as the prototype for the Leontini litra on the grounds of its ruder style. Although the coins

FIG. 2. Copenhagen, Ny Carlsberg Glyptotek: Bronze Statue Found in Rome

are typologically identical, they are utterly unlike stylistically, and the short, thick, cumbersome Stiela figure is rather to be explained as a derivation of the Leontini litra. The fact that, in other instances, the coinage of Stiela is extremely similar to superior types of Leontini and Catania, as K. Ziegler has pointed out (article "Stiela" in *R. E.*, sup. vol. VII, col. 1232 ff.), suggests that the coinage of Stiela was dependent upon those centres, and makes it highly improbable that Stiela inaugurated a type later picked up by Leontini. In this connection, see, too, note 43 of the Selinus-Pandosia discussion.

Fig. 3. Athens, National Museum: Bronze Statuette from Antikythera

14

II

THE HYPSAS didrachm issued by Selinus sometime between 466 and 409 B.C. is a coin of remarkable interest.[1] On its reverse, a youthful male figure stands beside an altar over which he holds a patera in his extended right hand (Pl. III, Fig. 1). His left hand grasps a short branch. To his left, a marsh bird stalks away, and the space above is filled by the famous σέλινον leaf. The inscription ΗΥΨΑΣ serves to identify the figure as the river god Hypsas whose waters flowed somewhat to the east of Selinus.

Like its predecessor, the tetradrachm of the

infected river by the philosopher Empedokles.[2] However, it has recently been demonstrated[3] that this established view is untenable and that, in all probability, the tetradrachm represents a sacred *temenos* in which we see not only a statue and an altar but a votive figure of a bull and, on some examples, a votive *pinakion*.[4] The selinon leaf itself may be such a simulacrum, given the well-known fact that the Selinuntines dedicated a golden representation of it in the temple of Apollo at Delphi. Surely some such object must have hung in the *temenos*. Indeed, the presence of the cock

FIG. 4. Lloyd Collection: Reverse of Tetradrachm of Selinus

river god Selinus (Fig. 4), this type has been interpreted as referring to sacrifices made in commemoration of the cleansing of the pestilence-

commonly found in connection with chthonic deities has evoked the specific suggestion that this tetradrachm gives an abbreviated representation

1. Hill, *Select Greek Coins*, pl. XXXIX, 3. [Pl. III, Fig. 1.]
2. For a summary of older explanations based upon Diogenes Laertius' account (VIII, 2, 70) of how Empedokles purified the pestilence-laden river, see A. H. Lloyd, "The Coin Types of Selinus and the Legend of Empedocles," *Num. Chr.*, ser. v, vol. XV, 1935, pp. 73 ff., pl. III–V, who pointed out that the topography of Selinus and the biography of Empedokles forbid such an explanation. S. Mirone, "Monnaies historiques de la Sicile antique," *Arethuse*, IV, 1927, p. 83 f. and Charles Picard, "Sur l'identification des temples de Sélinonte," *R. A.*, ser. VI, vol. VIII, 1936, pp. 23 ff., who interpreted the river gods as sacrificing to Apollo, and the cock and snake as "symboles sanitaires," accepted the Empedokles story. On p. 23, note 2, Picard quoted the article in the *Num. Chr.*, 1935, pp. 73 ff. as by Schwabacher instead of Lloyd, and said that in it "le rapport avec la mission d'Empedocle est signalé justement"— exactly the reverse of Lloyd's thesis. Lloyd's own explanation of the tetradrachm as representative of the union between Selinus and Himera (symbolized by the cock) against the common enemy

Akragas (present in the bull of Phalaris) is inventive but not convincing. His interpretation of the didrachm as a canting type in which the disdainful gait of the bird suggests conceit, a trait described by Greek words beginning with "υψ" and therefore used for Hypsas carries speculation too far. Present text Fig. 4 from Hill, *op. cit.*, pl. XL, 1.
3. By G. E. Rizzo, *Intermezzo*, pp. 49 ff. Rizzo attacked all previous symbolic interpretations of these coins and substituted very reasonable explanations based on facts indicated by the excavation of Selinus. Thus he connected the obverse of the tetradrachm with the local cult of Apollo in Temple G; the obverse of the didrachm with that of Herakles, considering this latter type to be derived from the official seal of the city known from seals excavated in Selinus. His explanations of the reverse sides are given above. Rizzo agreed with Lloyd's criticism of the older explanation but did not accept his alternate proposals.
4. *Ibid.*, fig. 15.

FIG. 1. London, British Museum: Reverse of Didrachm of Selinus

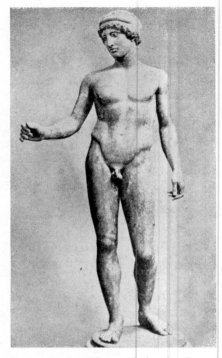

FIG. 2. Naples, Museo Nazionale: Bronze Statue from Pompeii

FIG. 3. Detail of FIG. 2

FIG. 4. Naples, Museo Nazionale: Bronze Statue from Pompeii

PLATE III

of the *temenos* of Demeter Malophoros whose sanctuary lay just west of the river Selinus who is therefore interpreted as doing honor to her.[5] Hence, the most reasonable explanation of the very similar Hypsas didrachm is that it, too, reproduces a *temenos*. But which *temenos* it is impossible to say, inasmuch as the snake coiled about the altar may indicate any of various chthonic divinities.[6] The marsh bird is apparently a purely numismatic addition intended to further characterize the river.

The identification of these figures as river gods has always rested upon the presence of their names and the assumption that the horns often characteristic of such divinities grow from their heads. Yet the supposed "horns" are strikingly unlike normal horns. The latter are well illustrated on the coinage of Gela, where they will be seen to grow from above the temples in a reverse curve.[7] On the contrary, the "horns" of both Selinus and Hypsas are not only single elements, but they spring directly from the centre of the forepart of the crown and are attached to a fillet. Clearly, it is not horns that these river gods wear but that variety of fillet having a long upright or apex in front which occurs on a number of contemporary monuments.[8]

The impression created by the coin type strongly reinforces the chief implication of this explanation, namely, that the coin type reproduces a statue of the river god Hypsas which stood in Selinus in the fifth century B.C. The beautifully preserved examples of this type give ample illustration of the appearance of that statue. And that such a statue existed is proven by a group of statues and statuettes intimately related to the didrachm type.

Foremost among these is the celebrated bronze statue found in Pompeii in 1925[9] (Pl. III, Figs. 2–4). Variously explained as a victorious young athlete pouring a libation,[10] a libation pourer,[11] a *lychnophoros* adapted from such earlier types,[12] and a Ganymede,[13] the Pompeii μελλέφηβος has evoked correspondingly divergent stylistic attributions, now to Pheidias[14] or his circle,[15] now to Alkamenes,[16] now to an Argive sphere[17] or, again, a neo-classical Athenian of the first century B.C.[18]

None of these stylistic attributions is convincing. The upholders of a Pheidian or near-Pheidian origin arrive at their conclusion primarily

5. *Ibid.*

6. Although, in the light of the Bibliothèque Nationale bronze discussed later, it is still tempting to consider this an altar to Asklepios. Former interpretations of the coin have considered that it represents a libation to the god of healing whose powers destroyed the baneful qualities of the marshland, thereby causing the marsh bird to withdraw. However, as yet, no trace of a cult of Asklepios has been found at Selinus.

7. See Hill, *op. cit.*, pl. III, No. 4 and Grose, pl. LXXII, Nos. 10–15, pl. LXXIII, No. 13. For additional illustrations of horns on coins see, for example, Hugo Gaebler, *Die antiken Münzen von Makedonia und Paionia (Die antiken Münzen Nord-Griechenlands, III)*, Berlin, 1935, III², pls. XXII, Nos. 24–25, XXXIII, Nos. 4–5.

8. I am greatly indebted to Miss Gisela M. A. Richter for calling my attention to this form of fillet. For bibliography on this subject see her *Red-Figured Athenian Vases*, New Haven, 1936, I, p. 128, note 12. For an interesting discussion of this type of fillet see G. Blum, "ΣΤΕΦΑΝΗ." *R.A.*, ser. IV, vol. XXI, 1913, pp. 269 ff. and especially p. 275 where its presence on the coinage of Selinus is noted. See, too, Eugen von Mercklin, "Antiken des R. Museo artistico industriale in Rom," *R. M.*, XXXVIII–XXXIX, 1923–24, pp. 86 ff., and pl. II¹.

9. Found in the atrium of a house on the Via dell' Abbondanza. Now in the Museo Nazionale in Naples. Ht: of figure: 1.49 m. Stands on moulded round base of Roman workmanship. Pupil and iris of eyes originally inlaid, now missing. Right arm detached at original joint; repaired. Right leg damaged at calf, left at knee. Traces of gilding visible on body. First published by A. Maiuri in *N. S.*, LII, 1927, pp. 63 ff. For the best photographs and a description of the excavation of the statue see Maiuri, "L'Efebo scoperto nei nuovi scavi di Pompei," *Antike Denkmäler*, Berlin, 1931, IV, pp. 43 ff.; for a shorter account, *idem*, *Pompeii*, Novara, 1929, pp. 74 ff.

10. Maiuri, "L'Efebo," p. 48 and S. Reinach, "L'Ephèbe pompéien," *G.B.A.*, LXVIII, 1926, pp. 193 ff.

11. G. E. Rizzo, "Copie romane della statua di bronzo scoperta a Pompei," *Bul. Com.*, LIII, 1925 (1926), pp. 13 ff.

12. C. Anti, "Il nuovo bronzo di Pompei," *Dedalo*, VII, 1926, pp. 73 ff.; A. Schober, "Zum neuen Epheben aus Pompeji," *Belvedere*, X, 1926, pp. 109 ff. Additional scholars cited later support this view.

13. W. Amelung, "Bronzener Ephebe aus Pompeji," *Jahrbuch*, XLII, 1927, pp. 137 ff. This position is accepted by Werner Technau, "Die Bronzestatue eines Knaben aus Pompeji," *Die Antike*, VI, 1930, Heft 3, pp. 259 ff.

14. Maiuri, "L'Efebo di Via dell'Abbondanza a Pompei," *B.d.A.* V, 1925–1926, pp. 343 ff. Later, in the *Antike Denkmäler* article quoted above, Maiuri modified this view and classed the statue as belonging to the Pheidian circle.

15. Reinach, *loc. cit.*

16. Sir Charles Walston, *Alcamenes*, Cambridge, 1926, pp. 217 ff.

17. Rizzo, Amelung, Technau, *loc. cit.*; Margarete Bieber, "Eine neue Bronzestatue aus Pompeji," *Nachrichten der Giessener Hochschulgesellschaft*, VI, 1, 1927, p. 33.

18. Anti and Schober, *loc. cit.* and H. Eckstein, "Eine neue Ephebenstatue," *Die Kunst für Alle*, XLII, 1926–27, pp. 37–39. Charles Picard, "La statue de bronze de Pompéi," *La revue de l'art*, L, 1926, pp. 113–116 leaned in this direction with his opinion that the statue is an Augustan copy. See, too, Ludwig Curtius, *Die antike Kunst (Handbuch der Kunstwissenschaft, II)*, Potsdam, 1938, pp. 247 ff.

because of the similarity between the head of the statue (Pl. III, Fig. 3) and the Bologna head of the Athena Lemnia. On the other hand, an Argive source is claimed for the youth by virtue of the supposedly Polykleitan tradition of the figure type and its relationship to such "Polykleitan" figures as the Idolino. The much-debated style of the Idolino, not to mention the absolutely un-Polykleitan head and wedge-shaped pelvis of the Pompeii statue, make such an attribution most unconvincing. The very divergence of these opinions has yielded a third, according to which the severe character of the head and the more advanced, more fluid rhythm of the figure are construed to indicate that the statue is a neo-classical pasticcio composed of a Pheidian head and a Polykleitan body. The latter theory makes no distinction in style and movement between the Via Abbondanza youth and the Porta Vesuvio figure found in Pompeii in 1900.[19] Yet nothing could be farther removed from the innate grace, the rhythmic unity, the artistic entity of the former than the startled forward stance, the staccato angularity, the jerky rhythm of the latter. The present orthodox concepts of regional and individual style afford no exit from this dilemma—unless it be that the very co-existence of stylistic elements not ordinarily found together smacks of a fine, yet judged by canonical standards, provincial style. In any case, the fact that at least six copies or variants are linked to the Via Abbondanza head[20] indicates the fame and popularity of the original upon which they all depend.

In my opinion, the obvious relationship between the Pompeii youth and the river god Hypsas provides the solution to this problem. A comparison of the two reveals an exact iconographic parallelism (Pl. III, Figs. 1, 2). The type and ponderation of the figure, the shapely legs, such a highly individual characteristic as the wide V-shape of the pelvis are identical on coin and statue. As nearly as can be determined from certain examples of the didrachm, Hypsas' long hair is tucked into the back of his fillet in exactly the fashion visible in the statue. In neither case is the ear visible. The separation of a patch of hair between the forehead and the tucked-up locks behind the ear on the didrachm heightens the probable identity. Equally close, in each case, is the proportion of hair to face and the long-nosed profile.

Given this remarkable degree of typological and stylistic similarity, it is reasonable to assume that statue and coin type alike reflect a common archetype—the original cult statue of the river god Hypsas.[21] Such minor differences as do exist between them are reconcilable. Chief among these is the greater twist in the torso of the coin type, an angularity probably largely caused by the difficulty of rendering in relief the slightly oblique direction of the body. Judging by the didrachm, the archetype must have been made about 450 B.C. The greater suavity of the bronze statue, its lack of similar emphasis on the muscles of the torso, points either to the die-cutter's retention of a somewhat antiquated anatomical symbol or device, or to a slight modification on the part of the copyist in the direction of the anatomical rendering practiced some twenty years later.[22] In addi-

19. Ruesch, *Guida illustrata del Museo Nazionale di Napoli*, No. 834, pp. 206 ff. The relationship between this statue and the group under discussion is stated on p. 27, note 41.
20. For a discussion of these copies see Rizzo, *op. cit.*, pp. 23 ff., who lists them in the following qualitative order: 1. Leningrad, O. Waldhauer, *Die antiken Skulpturen der Ermitage*, II, Berlin and Leipzig, 1931, p. 16, No. 106, pl. XVII, figs. 14–15. 2. Museo Barracco, No. 113, Helbig-Amelung, *Führer durch die öffentlichen Sammlungen klassicher Altertümer in Rom*, Leipzig, 3rd ed., 1912, I, p. 617, No. 1106. 3. Vatican, *ibid.*, No. 366. 4. Rome, Museo Nazionale, No. 523, R. Paribeni, "Incrementi del Museo Nazionale Romano," *B.d.A.*, IV, 1910, pp. 307 ff. and fig. 1. 5. Naples, Museo Nazionale, Ruesch, *Guida illustrata*, I, p. 49, No. 143. 6. Formerly in the Villa Ludovisi, now in Copenhagen, *Ny-Carlsberg Glyptotek. Tillaeg til Billedtavler af antike Kunstvaerker*, Copenhagen, 1915, pl. XXIV, No. 345.

21. Rizzo, *op. cit.*, pp. 35 ff., in sketching the evolution of the *offerente* type, noted the typological relationship of the Pompeii statues and the Selinus coins. Apparently, his opinion—that it would be an unscientific procedure insufficiently bolstered by examples to consider that the coin type reflected any given statue—prevented him from pursuing this observation to its logical conclusion. I hope that the present application of the method will help to remove skepticism in regard to its reliability. Rizzo was certainly right in considering the Agrigento youth as a forerunner of the Hypsas-Pandosia type, and the Selinus, Aderno, and Louvre bronzes, the Idolino and the Sabouroff figures as related in one way or another to this general type of *offerente*. Such of these statues as are actually related to the Hypsas type will be considered in the present discussion. Those that are either prototypes (Agrigento) or reverse the stance (Selinus) are not considered here.
22. The stylistic development of a fixed type has long been noted in connection with the Selinuntine coin types. Cf., especially, Julius Lange, *Darstellung des Menschen in der älteren griechischen Kunst*, Strassburg, 1899, pp. 96–98. Here, too, Lange suggested the possibility of a plastic prototype behind the numismatic type. For further discussion of this point see note 40.

tion, the upright unit of Hypsas' fillet, and possibly the position of the right fingers, separate the coin type from the bronze. Inasmuch as the latter is linked with the final use of the Pompeii statue, it is well to review its history.

Two curving candelabra stems found with the statue, together with traces of gilding visible on the body, indicated that the youth had served as a *lychnophoros*[23] (Pl. III, Fig. 4). In the course of adapting the river god to this purpose, it may have been necessary to modify his right hand slightly in order to facilitate the insertion of the candelabra support. Certain scholars[24] have considered that in its present condition the hand could only hold a *kantharos*. Yet a comparison with enlarged illustrations of the coin indicates that even the present position would be possible for the grasping of a patera. Whichever stand one takes in this matter, the fact remains that the insertion of brackets would be sufficient to account for any modification made to the hand of the Pompeii statue. Thus the original figure may be restored with the patera and the short laurel branch of the coin.

When this adaptation took place it is impossible to say. Several alternatives exist: the Pompeii statue may be a contemporary copy of the archetype, in which case it may have been adapted to serve as a *lychnophoros* either immediately or centuries later when it stood in the house of a Roman collector; or it may be a later copy intentionally reproducing a famous statue in a manner calculated to appeal to contemporary taste.[25] But

that the entire figure is a neo-classical creation conceived from the beginning for use as a *lychnophoros*[26] is hardly possible. The stylistic arguments cited above, the improbability that a *lychnophoros* would have been perpetuated in marble copies,[27] and the simple fact that a less convenient position of the arms—especially of the relaxed left arm—could scarcely be devised for the purpose of holding heavy supports all preclude such an explanation.[28] On the other hand, the adaptability of such an offering type to this purpose is undeniable. Finally, Hesiod's description of the River Gods as similar to Apollo in their capacity as protectors of youth[29] throws light on both the original conception of Hypsas as a boy, and on the appropriateness of such a type as a model for any figure in which a youth was required or desirable.[30]

The remaining reflections of the Hypsas archetype are bronze statuettes of the classical period. Although greatly inferior in quality to the splendid Pompeii statue, they are of interest in reconstructing the nature and influence of the arche-

23. For photographs of the figure holding these tendrils and for further details cf. *Antike Denkmäler, loc. cit.*
24. Notably Amelung, *loc. cit.*; hence his explanation of the figure as Ganymede.
25. The fact that the statue stands on a Roman base may be an argument in favor of its having undergone a quite considerable renovation before 79 A.D., a renovation in which the statue was both transformed into a *lychnophoros* and given a new base. However, once the type was established as a *lychnophoros*, it was repeated in genuinely neo-classical works. Such is the bronze statue of a youth found in a villa at Volubilis and now in the local museum. Ht: 1.40 m. (E. Michon, "Ephèbe couronné," *Fondation Piot, Monuments et Mémoires*, XXXIII, 1933, pp. 119–134.) Michon's interpretation of the statue as a *lychnophoros* seems reasonable, if not inevitable, and, given details like the extreme naturalism of the ivy crown in comparison with the greater severity of the head, a late date in the first century B.C. is required. However, Michon's chief arguments for this attribution are identical with those of Anti with whom he agrees in regard to the eclectic combination of Attic and Argive features—arguments

that have been considered above. Whether the Volubilis boy is a variant of the archetype or of the Pompeii version, it is not possible to say.
26. The position of A. Rumpf, "Der Idolino," *La critica d'arte*, IV, 1939, pp. 17 ff. See also the discussion of the Idolino in the latter part of this chapter.
27. That none of the copies, including those from which these marble heads come, preserved that minor detail, the upright part of the fillet is present in the archetype, is not surprising.
28. Walston, *loc. cit.*, noted this same point.
29. *Theogony*, 346–348. F. Matz, too (*Die Naturpersonificationen in der griechischen Kunst*, Göttingen, 1913, p. 111), says that "wo der Flussgott als Schützer der männlichen Jugend, als Förderer ihres Wachstums und ihrer Kraft dargestellt werden sollte, sehr nahe lag, ihn selbst sich als das ideale Vorbild zu denken und als blühenden Knaben zu gestalten." For bibliography and a lengthy discussion of river gods see the article "Flussgötter" by Waser in *R.E.*, VI, cols. 2774 ff.
30. The marked similarities which the Sabouroff statue (A. Furtwängler, *La collection Sabouroff*, pls. VIII–XI and text; now in Berlin, *Führer durch das Antiquarium*, I, p. 18, pl. XXXIX) presents to this type suggest that it is the work of a later artist belonging to a different school, who utilized the iconographic type of the Hypsas archetype in devising a youthful Apollo.

Two bronze statuettes reproduced in Reinach, *Répertoire*, II¹, p. 85, No. 2, p. 507, No. 7 appear to be typologically related to the works under discussion. Whether they, too, illustrate the use of this type by different schools or, in fact, exactly what their specific stylistic relationship to the group may be cannot be determined from the Reinach drawings. Still another reflection of the type is to be found in a bronze statuette published in the *Bulletin de l'institut archéologique bulgare*, II, 1923–24, p. 228, fig. 107.

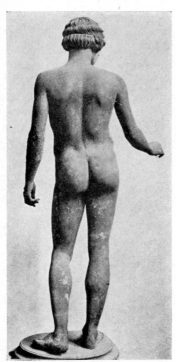

FIG. 5. Naples, Museo Nazionale:
Rear View of Bronze Statue from
Pompeii

FIG. 6. Former Somzée Collection: Bronze Mirror Handle

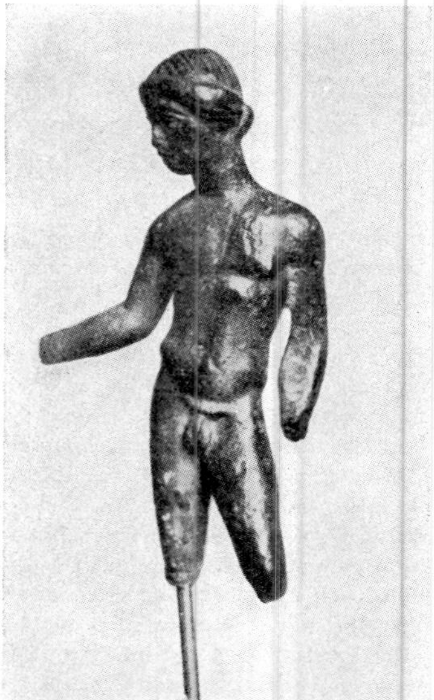

FIG. 8. Budapest Museum: Bronze
Statuette

FIG. 7. Paris, Bibliothèque Nationale: Bronze Statuette Found in Bologna

PLATE IV

type. Among them is a bronze mirror handle from the Somzée collection[31] (Pl. IV, Fig. 6). The general characteristics of the coin type, both typological and stylistic, are repeated save for the apparent modification of the right forearm; the same rather hip-shot, elongated figure, the same wedge-shaped pelvis and shapely legs. Even the coarse rendering of the coiffure reflects a similar, if schematically shown, style of hairdressing. A comparison of a rear view of the statuette with the head of the Pompeii figure (Pl. III, Fig. 3) proves the point.[32] Indeed, this modified version of the archetype is quite close to the Pompeii statue in the modelling of both the torso and the legs (cf. Pl. IV, Figs. 5, 6), despite the fact that it probably constitutes a somewhat later version of the statue.[33]

A further variant of the archetype is to be found in a bronze statuette in the Bibliothèque Nationale in Paris[34] (Pl. IV, Fig. 7). The youthful figure stands in an attitude identical with that of all the figures previously discussed. The ponderation of the figure, the angle of the extended right arm,

and the hole running through the left hand guarantee the restoration of a patera and lustral branch as the missing attributes. Stylistically, the statuette is inferior to the preceding examples, being of cruder workmanship, and it differs from them not only in its more schematized rendering of the torso but also in its hairdress. For the hair, although bound by a fillet, escapes in one broad strand which hangs down the back of the neck. Hence the statuette is a variant reflecting the iconographic characteristics of the archetype. Its chief interest, however, is the inscription preserved on its legs: along the right leg Αἰσχλαβίοι, along the left, Καφισόδορος. The letters are of Corinthian character, a style used by Corinth, Megara, and their colonies, including Selinus.[35] Under these circumstances, the inscription, too, offers a strong argument in favor of the contemporary Selinuntine workmanship of the statuette and of its dependence iconographically, at least, upon the Hypsas archetype.[36] Its Bolognese provenance, pointing toward an Italian origin for the piece, constitutes a final reinforcement of this attribution.

This inscription arouses the old question of whether the snake coiled about the altar on the didrachms really should be interpreted as indicative of Asklepios. Certainly, if a statue sacrificing before an altar to Asklepios was duplicated in small votive copies, nothing would be more likely than that they, too, would be used as dedications to Asklepios. Although the question cannot be answered conclusively, the evidence afforded by the Paris statuette revives the likelihood of the old explanation.

31. A. Furtwängler, *Collection Somzée*, Munich, 1897, No. 84, pp. 55 ff., pl. XXXII. Ht: 10 cm. Light green patina. Mouth and nose somewhat worn; lacks left hand, forepart of left foot, entire right foot. Rumor alone had it that the provenance was Peloponnesian. Hence it may be discarded.

32. *Ibid.*, pl. XXXII and *Antike Denkmäler, loc. cit.*, figs. 7, 8 and pl. XXIX.

33. Furtwängler, *op. cit.*, considered the Somzée bronze to be a reproduction of a lost work of art known in a marble copy in Cassel (Margarete Bieber, *Die antiken Skulpturen und Bronzen des Königl. Museum Friedericianum in Cassel*, Marburg, 1915, No. 9, pl. XVI, pp. 12–13). Ht: without base: 0.98 m. Of close-grained, possibly Pentelic marble. Yellow-white patina. Restored: right leg including prop up to break; left foot and joint; break under left knee; lacks head and neck, right arm below biceps, left forearm, forepart of penis. Although the youthful, slender proportions of the figure and its ponderation are in favor of such a connection, the modelling of the torso, and especially the more conventional shape of the pelvis present difficulties which can only be overcome by the assumption that they are modifications made by a classicizing Roman copyist—a statement that, in the present case, cannot be flatly made. However, the similarities do remain, as does the possibility that the Cassel figure may constitute a free Roman rendering of the Hypsas archetype. Furtwängler considered that the head formerly exhibited with this torso belonged to it. Cf. Bieber, *op. cit.*, No. 3, pl. XIV, pp. 8–9. More recent examination (*ibid.*) indicates that the two cannot belong together. For a different opinion about the torso cf. Bieber, *loc. cit.*

34. No. 98. Ht: 0.148 m. Right hand and attribute of left hand missing. Brown patina. Found in Bologna in the mid-seventeenth century when the foundations for the Palazzo Ranuzzi were dug. For an extensive bibliography on the figure see Babelon and Blanchet, *Catalogue des bronzes antiques de la Bibliothèque Nationale*, pp. 45 ff.

35. Quoted as belonging to this group in the article on *Asklepios* by Thraemer in *R.E.*, II, col. 1642. See also A. Kirchhoff, *Studien zur Geschichte des griechischen Alphabets*, Gütersloh, 1887, p. 113. The inscription itself is published in *C.I.G.*, XIV, No. 2282. Furtwängler, *op. cit.*, recognized the relationship between the Somzée and Bibliothèque Nationale bronzes. On the basis of the reputed Peloponnesian provenance of the former and the Corinthian characters of the latter, he considered this entire group Corinthian and made their common coiffure a Corinthian characteristic. Not connecting any of the figures with Selinus, he had no occasion to investigate the possibility that the Paris bronze might come from a colony using the Corinthian alphabet.

36. Jantzen, *Bronzewerkstätten in Grossgriechenland und Sizilien*, p. 64 attributed the Paris bronze to Tarentum because of its supposedly Peloponnesian figure type. This statement is unfounded, since Jantzen neither discussed the problem raised by the inscription nor mentioned nor refuted any previous opinions in regard to the statuette.

Closely related to the preceding figure is another small bronze statuette in Budapest (Pl. IV, Fig. 8).[37] Iconographically identical, it is even closer to the coin type than the Paris statuette, being slimmer and more angular, and in its coiffure exactly like the Somzée bronze (Pl. IV, Fig. 6). Hence it may be considered an additional reflection of the once famous archetype.[38]

Thus the sculpturesque appearance of the Hypsas didrachm, and its interpretation as a reproduction of a lost statue of the river god produced about 450 B.C., is vindicated. The fame of this bronze archetype must have been widespread since it is preserved not only in the life-size Pompeii copy, in marble heads and bronze statuettes dependent upon it, but, in addition, it motivated later *lychnophoroi* like the Volubilis youth and such a related iconographic type as the Sabouroff Apollo.[39] Finally, as the following discussion will show, it stimulated the creation of similar plastic and numismatic works.[40]

37. Ht: 7 cm. Lacks both hands and both legs below the knees. Published by Langlotz, *Frühgriechische Bildhauerschulen*, p. 81, pl. 42 D, who, apparently chiefly on the basis of Furtwängler's remarks about this type of coiffure, attributed it to Corinth.

38. An additional reflection of the archetype is to be seen in the iconographically similar bronze statuette standing on an Ionic capital ornamenting the top of a bronze candelabrum found in a late fifth- or early fourth-century tomb near Kertsch (*Compterendu de la commission impériale archéologique pour l'année 1877*, St. Petersburg, 1880, pp. 221 ff., especially pp. 226 ff.; Atlas, pl. III, Nos. 17, 18). Judging by the old illustration, the style of this figure differs considerably from the archetype. Without a photograph, it is impossible to determine the style or weigh the likelihood of the figure's having been imported into this region. For a further discussion of the use to which the type was adapted here see p. 27, note 37.

The basic formal and typological similarity underlying the Pompeii statute and the well-known relief of Antinous-Silvanus from Torre del Padiglione in the Istituto di Fondi Rustici in Rome is so marked as to suggest the possibility that in creating an appropriate type for this fusion of the beautiful favorite and an elderly god of fertility, the sculptor was influenced by the Hypsas archetype or one of its copies. Both the youth and nature of the river god would have lent themselves to such an application. For a discussion of the relief see G. E. Rizzo, "Antinoo-Silvano," *Ausonia*, III, 1908, pp. 3–17, pl. I; *idem*, in Br.-Br., No. 635; E. S. Strong, *La scultura romana*, Florence, 1923, pl. XLIII, and Georg Lippold, *Kopien und Umbildungen griechischer Statuen*, Munich, 1923, p. 193, where a statuary prototype for the relief is also suggested. For additional bibliography see P. Marconi, "Antinoo: Saggio sull'arte dell'età adrianea," *Monumenti antichi*, XXIX, 1923, p. 175 and Jocelyn M. C. Toynbee, *The Hadrianic School*, Cambridge, 1934, p. 242, v.

39. The type is also echoed on Roman coins and gems (see, for example, the two gems published on successive pages by P. S. Bartoli, *Raccolta di varie antichità e lucerne antiche*, Rome, *ca.* 1690. I am indebted to Karl Lehmann for calling these gems to my attention) where it is identified as Bonus Eventus. Inasmuch as Pliny mentioned a bronze statue by Euphranor of Bonus Eventus (i.e. Agathos Daimon or Triptolemos) holding a patera in his right hand and corn and poppies in the left, Furtwängler, *Masterpieces*, pp. 349 ff. interpreted this Roman type as a reflection of Euphranor's statue. See, too, A. B. Cook, *Zeus*, Cambridge, II², 1925, pp. 1126 ff. The gem type certainly looks more fifth than fourth century in derivation. Hence, if Furtwängler's combination is correct, Euphranor may have adapted an earlier fifth-century statuary type for his image, since the analogy between these coins and the Hypsas type is obvious. In this case, we might have a parallel to Lysippos' adaptation of a fifth-century Herakles type for his Herakles Epitrapezios as proposed below, pp. 40 ff.

40. The Selinus tetradrachm has been described above as an abbreviated representation of a *temenos* containing an image of the river god Selinus. Given the date of the coin in conjunction with the movement of the figure, it is likely that the type is a purely imaginative rendering of the characteristic attributes and action of the god in his sanctuary—whichever one it may have been— and that it was conceived of in the two dimensional terms of vase painting (a comparison already made by Rizzo, *Intermezzo, loc. cit.*) rather than as the reproduction of a contemporary statue. At the most, the numismatic type may indicate that a statue carrying a patera and a branch stood in the sanctuary. This interpretation of the type is strongly reinforced by the fact that the search for a comparable statue has not yielded any results. However, once this religious concept led to the creation of an actual statue of the river god Hypsas, that statue, as we have seen, was reproduced as the didrachm type, probably as a result of the existence and influence of the now-established iconography of the tetradrachm type. Finally, the didrachm type appears to have influenced the later numismatic variants of the tetradrachm. (Cf. Hill, *Select Greek Coins*, pl. XLI, 5 where the river god on a late example of the tetradrachm plainly appears as a statue standing on a base). This interpretation of the creation and interrelation of the tetradrachms and didrachms is confirmed by W. Schwabacher's study of the die-sequences of the tetradrachm ("Die Tetradrachmenprägung von Selinunt," *Mitteilungen der bayerischen numismatischen Gesellschaft*, XLIII, 1925, pp. 1–89). He divides the dies into four periods: the striding type of 467–445 being succeeded by the himation type of 445–435, followed by a return to the nude type in modernized versions from 435–417, and concluding in the late issues of 417–409, one of which shows a *pinax* in the field. On purely numismatic grounds, he dates the Hypsas didrachm a decade later than the earliest tetradrachms (p. 71), and considers that the later dies of Period I reflect the influence of the first new didrachms (p. 42). Although this is admittedly a relative stylistic chronology checked against historical data, it is the sequence of the types that is of particular interest in the present instance. Note that on p. 78, Schwabacher speaks of "das rein statuarische Flussgottmotiv."

For comment on a proposed association of the bronze statue from Castelvetrano with the early tetradrachm type, see p. 11.

III

OBVIOUSLY related to this Selinuntine type is the somewhat later stater issued by Pandosia in Bruttium[1] (Pl. v, Fig. 9). This inland town, situated near the river Krathis, is thought to have struck coins only in the second half of the fifth century.[2] A date somewhere around 430 B.C. seems stylistically appropriate for the type.[3] The river god Krathis, as the inscription indicates, is shown as a nude youth standing with his weight on his right leg, his left being at ease. In his extended right hand he holds a patera. A tall laurel branch lightly held in his left hand leans against his shoulder.[4]

Although the figure differs from the Hypsas type in certain details—the lower angle of the right arm, the placing and attribute of the left arm, the greater freedom of the left leg, the more advanced rendering of the lean, flat, markedly hip-shot body—the basic similarity is so great as to indicate that the Krathis type must have been derived from the Hypsas (cf. Pl. III, Fig. 1 and Pl. v, Fig. 9). This similarity might simply be the result of a numismatic dependence of the Pandosia stater on the Selinus didrachm. In this case, no statuary type need lie behind the statuesque-looking Krathis. One factor makes such an explanation unlikely: the existence of plastic works iconographically and stylistically identical with the Krathis type. Apparently, it, too, reproduces a

statue.[5] The fact remains that a relationship does exist between the archetypes of the Pandosia stater and the Selinus didrachm. Its nature will be defined later.[6]

A comparison of the Pandosia stater and the famous bronze statue found in Pesaro in 1530 and long known as the Idolino (Pl. v, Figs. 10–11) yields results of remarkable interest.[7] Not only the general iconography of the coin is duplicated in the statue but the curious ponderation of the Idolino whereby the youth stands with his weight emphatically cast on his right leg while his left foot is placed to the side in a highly individual fashion giving to the figure its strange angularity, its concentration of stress on the right hip from which the diagonals of the torso and left leg spring is exactly repeated on the coin. And again, not only are coin and statue alike in this angularity of ponderation and in the narrow, flat, slender forms of the body, but such details as the angle of the extended arm, the silhouette of the taut right side and the five major curves of the relaxed left torso and leg, the modelling of the torso with its V-shaped pelvis—all are identical. Unfortunately, the worn surface of the stater prevents certain details from being sharply visible; but, apparently, the river god Krathis is similarly short-haired.

1. Obv: ΠΑΝΔΟΣΙΑ (in archaic letters); head of nymph Pandosia wearing broad diadem; the whole in laurel wreath. Rev: ΚΡΑΘΙΣ (in archaic letters). At feet of the river god, a fish. In the Head *Guide*, pl. XIV, 19, p. 25, the inconsistency of the style of the type in comparison with that of the letters is considered proof that the latter reflect "an affectation of archaism." Head, *H.N.*, p. 106 had viewed this archaic lettering as an argument for dating the type earlier, i.e., before 443 and the appearance of the ordinary forms of the alphabet on the coinage of Sybaris. Present Pl. v, Fig. 9 from Gardner, *The Types of Greek Coins*, pl. I, 17.
2. Head, *H.N.*, p. 105.
3. Precisely the date suggested by Gardner, *The Types of Greek Coins*, p. 100. Schwabacher, *op. cit.*, p. 74 dated the unique example in the British Museum approximately 435 B.C.
4. A. J. Evans, "Contributions to Sicilian Numismatics. II," *Num. Chr.*, ser. III, vol. XVI, 1896, p. 126, note 64, very reasonably pointed out that the sacred trees of river gods would naturally be those growing on their banks. As an indication of the place these divinities occupied in local worship, he, too, recalled Plutarch's statement (*Nikias*, XXVII, 6; XXVIII, 1) that after the Syracusan victory over the Athenians at Asinaros, the conquerors' trophies were hung on the tallest trees by the river in whose name a festival was forthwith instituted.
5. Mirone, "Copies de statues sur les monnaies de la Grande Grèce," *R.N.*, ser. IV, vol. XXVIII, 1925, p. 15, although apparently unaware of the relationship of the Krathis to the Selinus types and of the existence of related sculptures, cited this coin as copied from a statue. For comment on his method see p. 2, note 10.
6. It is hardly necessary to go into Charles Waldstein's confused suggestions ("Pythagoras of Rhegion and the Early Athletic Statues," *J.H.S.*, II, 1881, pp. 349 ff. reprinted as an appendix to *Essays on the Art of Phidias*, Cambridge, 1885, pp. 370–371) about the dependence of the Selinus and Pandosia types upon athletic statues like his pugilist-Omphalos Apollo.
7. Ht: 1.48 m.; eyes and incrustation of lips lacking; right arm has been broken and repaired; no soles to feet, indicating that statue originally stood on a stone base with lead fastening. Technique and patina of present base different. Found by a native of Pesaro in the fall of 1530 and presented to Francesco Maria of Urbino; stood in the Villa Imperiale till 1633, when it passed to Florence at the marriage of Vittoria, niece of the last Rovere, and Ferdinand II. Now in the Museo Archeologico, Florence. Br.-Br., Nos. 274–277; W. Amelung, *Führer durch die Antiken in Florenz*, Munich, 1897, No. 268, p. 272; L. A. Milani, *Il Reggio Museo Archeologico di Firenze*, Florence, 1912, I, p. 173; II, pl. CXLIII. For the most complete bibliography see A. Rumpf, "Der Idolino," *La critica d'arte*, IV, 1939, pp. 17 ff.

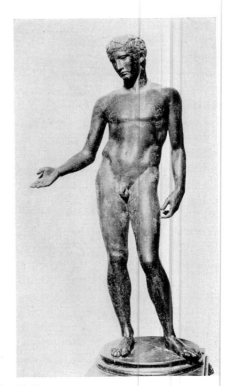

FIGS. 10–11. Florence, Museo Archeologico: Bronze Statue Found in Pesaro, the Idolino

FIG. 9. London, British Museum: Reverse of Stater of Pandosia

FIG. 12. New York, Metropolitan Museum of Art: Bronze Statuette

PLATE V

Before entering into a discussion of the implications arising from this degree of similarity or attempting to define the nature of the Idolino, it may be well to recall the conflicting identifications and attributions evoked by the figure. Long considered an original of the fifth century, it has of late been called a Roman copy thanks to the discovery of a partially preserved basalt head in the storerooms of the Vatican.[8] This head is clearly derived from a bronze prototype—either the Idolino itself or its original—and is thought to indicate that the Idolino, too, is a similar, if more faithful, derivation.[9] In the course of its long history, the Idolino has been interpreted as a Bacchus,[10] a *deus praestes*,[11] a Hermes,[12] an Apollo,[13] a youthful Herakles,[14] a boy victor sacrificing,[15] a divine libation pourer,[16] and a *lychno-phoros*.[17] It has been emphatically described as Myronic,[18] Attic,[19] Polykleitan or from the circle of Polykleitos[20] or Argive,[21] as conceivably by Patrokles,[22] or an artist working in the second half of the fifth century and influenced by both Polykleitos and contemporary Attic masters;[23] as Pheidian,[24] as a work of the school of Kleonai[25] or of the early fourth century[26] and, finally, as a neo-classical Augustan statue.[27] The very range of these identifications and attributions attests the difficulty of accepting any of them.

Of the stylistic attributions, those to the circle of Polykleitos or to an artist strongly influenced by him have predominated. They have been arrived at primarily through consideration of the marked affinities between the head of the Idolino and such Polykleitan works as the Doryphoros and the Westmacott athlete. Yet, the obvious discrepancy between the body of the Idolino and normal Polykleitan works forced some scholars to remove the statue from the immediate circle of the Argive master. Furtwängler, especially, considered the position of the left leg, the angle made by the left arm, the wiry, spare forms of the body

8. See G. Kaschnitz-Weinberg, *Sculture del magazzino del Museo Vaticano*, Vatican City, 1937, No. 60, pp. 39 ff., Pls. xix–xx for a discussion of this head and its discovery by Amelung. Considered to be a first-century B.C., possibly early Augustan, copy. Kaschnitz' opinion that the Idolino is a copy is shared, for example, by Lippold, *op. cit.*, p. 125, Gerhart Rodenwaldt, *Olympia*, New York, 1936, p. 49, and Curtius, *Die antike Kunst*, p. 260.

9. Theoretically, it is not impossible that both an original and a copy could survive from antiquity. The ultimate decision, in the present case, must rest on an examination of the technique of the bronze-casting. It is interesting to note, therefore, that according to Karl Lehmann the late Kurt Kluge considered that the technical differences between the Idolino and Roman bronzes pointed toward its being a Greek original.

10. The original interpretation found in documents contemporary with its discovery and quoted by R. Kekulé, "Über die Bronzestatue des sogenannten Idolino," *Neunundvierzigstes Programm zum Winckelmannsfeste*, Berlin, 1899, p. 3. The report that the head was crowned with vine leaves and grapes and that the hand held a vine tendril at the time of its discovery probably led to the statue's being interpreted as Bacchus. This interpretation, in turn, appears to have determined the Bacchic iconography of the beautiful Renaissance base on which the statue now stands. (For recent discussion of the style of this base see, for example, Ulrich Middeldorf, "Notes on Italian Bronzes," *The Burlington Magazine*, LXXII–LXXIII, 1938, pp. 251–253; C. F. Bell, "Sergel and Neo-Classicism," *The Burlington Magazine*, LXXXIV–LXXXV, 1944, p. 97, and F. J. B. Watson, "On the Early History of Collecting in England," pp. 227 ff. of the same volume. I am indebted to Clarence Kennedy for these references.) F. de Clarac, *Musée de sculpture*, Paris, IV, 1836–37, p. 195 and pl. 680, No. 1591, quoted but rejected this identification.

11. A. F. Gori, *Statuae antiquae deorum et virorum illustrium* (*Museum Florentinum*, III), Florence, 1734, pp. 49 ff. and pls. XLV–XLVI. Cf. Johann Winckelmann, *Geschichte der Kunst des Alterthums*, Dresden, 1764, I, p. 93. For other early interpretations of the Idolino see Kekulé, *op. cit.*, pp. 4 ff.

12. E. Q. Visconti, *Museo Pio-Clementino*, Rome, 1782–1807, II, p. 184, note 2 and Lange, *op. cit.*, p. 219, note 1.

13. L. A. Milani, *N.S.*, XII, 1887, p. 226.

14. J. N. Svoronos, *Das Athener Nationalmuseum*, II, pp. 416 ff.

15. Amelung, Milani, Kekulé, *loc. cit.* C. Friedrichs, *Berlins antike Bildwerke*, Berlin, II, 1871, p. 453, note 1; H. Bulle, *Der schöne Mensch im Altertum*, Munich and Leipzig, 1911, cols. 105–106; P. Ducati, *L'Arte classica*, Turin, 1927, p. 325; E. N. Gardiner, *Athletics of the Ancient World*, Oxford, 1930, fig. 14; E. Buschor, *Die Plastik der Griechen*, Berlin, 1936, pp. 76 ff.; Rodenwaldt, *op. cit.*, p. 49; C. Blümel, *Sport der Hellenen*, Berlin, 1936, p. 10, No. 5, p. 113.

16. Furtwängler, *Masterpieces*, pp. 283 ff.

17. Rumpf, *loc. cit.*

18. Kekulé, *op. cit.*, p. 12; H. Schrader, *Phidias*, Frankfurt a.M., 1924, p. 71. Cf. Franz Studniczka, "Zum Myronischen Diskobol," *Festschrift für Otto Benndorf*, Vienna, 1898, p. 175, and Wilhelm Klein, *Geschichte der griechischen Kunst*, Leipzig, 1905, II, pp. 30–31 who inclined to attribute the Idolino to Myron's son.

19. Svoronos, Bieber, Ducati, Bulle, *loc. cit.*; A. Conze, *Beiträge zur Geschichte der griechischen Plastik*, Halle, 1869, p. 27.

20. Arndt, Buschor, *loc. cit.*; Lange, *op. cit.*, pp. 217 ff.; Curtius, Br.-Br., No. 567, pp. 6 ff. and *Die antike Kunst*, pp. 195 ff.; Lippold, *op. cit.*, pp. 125–126; E. Pfuhl, "Artemis von Ariccia, Athena von Velletri und die Amazonen," *Jahrbuch*, XLI, 1926, p. 36; Schober, *op. cit.*, p. 111; G. M. A. Richter, *The Sculpture and Sculptors of the Greeks*, New York, 1930, p. 251.

21. Pfuhl, *loc. cit.* Cf. Kaschnitz-Weinberg, *op. cit.*, p. 40.

22. Furtwängler, *loc. cit.*

23. Amelung, *op. cit.*, p. 274. Cf. W. W. Hyde, *Olympic Victor Monuments and Greek Athletic Art*, Washington, 1921, pp. 141 ff.

24. A. Mahler, *Polyklet und seine Schule*, Athens and Leipzig, 1902, pp. 70 ff.

25. Langlotz, *op. cit.*, pp. 68 ff.

26. H. K. Süsserott, *Griechische Plastik des 4. Jahrhunderts vor Christus*, Frankfurt a.M., 1938, pp. 137 ff.

27. Rumpf, *loc. cit.*

and, above all, the acute angle of the abdomen, as absolutely un-Polykleitan[28]—several of the exact respects, be it noted, in which the statue is akin to the Pandosia coin type. In the face of this obvious discrepancy, the Idolino cannot be Polykleitan, nor is it convincing to attribute it to a hypothetical personality like Patrokles. At the most, a certain Polykleitan influence remains.

On the basis of this "discrepancy," a new "pasticcio" explanation comparable to that of the Via Abbondanza youth has arisen.[29] Its author, starting on the assumption that this entire group of statues was designed to be viewed from a three-quarter angle, proceeds to bolster his position by stating that it was not characteristic of classical art to present figures at an oblique angle although such was the Roman practice—hence the statue is Augustan![30] That a work as individual in ponderation, as harmonious in style as the Idolino should be consigned to a neo-classic atelier simply because, despite its clear evidence of Polykleitan influence, it cannot be placed within the master's circle, is the result of fallacious reasoning. As in the case of the Via Abbondanza bronze, no theoretical obstacle stands in the way of attributing such a piece to any master somewhat influenced by Polykleitan style. And if that master's style fits into no clearly recognized artistic milieu, the problem must remain unsolved unless objective facts or similarities can be found which afford an explanation. Just such an objective fact is the typological and stylistic similarity of the Idolino

and the Pandosia stater.[31] Before discussing this relationship further, let us consider the interpretation of the figure.

Of the opinions quoted above, the most commonly accepted view—that the Idolino is a victor statue—has persisted in spite of Furtwängler's emphatic statement that although mortal boys *serve* libations, they never perform the ritual act of pouring them, with the result that the Idolino must represent a divine, not a mortal youth.[32] For it is agreed that only a shallow bowl like a patera would fit into the flat, open, right hand. Exactly which god or *daimon* the Idolino represented, Furtwängler felt unable to determine. Yet, interestingly enough, he considered the river god Hypsas on the coinage of Selinus an analogous figure, just as other scholars have been sufficiently struck by this resemblance to use the coin as the basis for restoring a patera and lustral branch to the statue.[33] In these iconographic respects, the Hypsas didrachm and the Krathis stater are identical.

The latest and most radical opinion,[34] that the Idolino is an Augustan *pasticcio* designed from the beginning as a *lychnophoros*, is based both upon its present affinity to the similar figures discussed previously, and on the belief that originally the Idolino was accompanied by tendrils similar to those found with the Pompeii figure. To be sure, the earliest document states that:

sub terram per pedes circiter decem reperta est statua Aenea Bacchi antiquissima frondibus et vitium fructibus circa tempora ornata: que in altera manuum frondosam vitem cum uvarum racemis habet statque supra basim.[35]

This passage indicates that the Idolino wore a wreath about its head and carried vine tendrils

---

28. Bulle, too, *loc. cit.*, stressed the individual character of this style.

29. Rumpf, *loc. cit.*

30. Rumpf's criticism of the aesthetic quality of the figure when seen from his arbitrarily established viewpoint is scarcely convincing. To other eyes, the overlapping of forms created by this viewpoint—as left hand over left thigh, right side over right arm—seems far more unclassical than the clear outlines of the figure seen almost frontally. (According to Karl Lehmann, the upper part of the right arm was deformed in the Renaissance restoration; originally, it may not have been so sharply separated from the chest.) The very analogy between the position of the feet when seen frontally and fifth-century vase painting led Kekulé, *loc. cit.*, to consider the frontal view of the Idolino the aspect from which it was intended to be seen. Even if the Idolino were not as intimately related to the Pandosia and, through it, to the Selinus coin types as it apparently is, its general similarity to those coins would be sufficient to indicate that they afford by far the best guide as to the proper angle from which the figure should be seen. The resulting viewpoint is radically different from Rumpf's proposed correct angle.

31. Rizzo's complaint, *op. cit.*, p. 50, that insufficient knowledge of Greek art has given rise to the prejudice that everything fine and delicate is Attic might be paraphrased to read that every good piece found in Italy must have been imported from Greece.

32. *Loc. cit.*

33. Cf. Kekulé, *op. cit.*, p. 8; Lange, *op. cit.*, pp. 217 ff.

34. Rumpf, *loc. cit.*

35. Quoted by Kekulé, *op. cit.*, p. 15, who repudiated the reports. Rumpf, *loc. cit.*, is quite right in stating that such attributes cannot be dismissed as Renaissance additions since they are not in character with the Renaissance concept of Bacchus. For a review of the history of these attributes see Rumpf's article. Rudolf Hallo, "Bronzeabgüsse antiker Statuen," *Jahrbuch*, XLII, 1927, pp. 206 ff. mentioned an early eighteenth-century cast of the Idolino bearing traces of a screw hole in the interior of the left hand where the tendril was attached.

26

in its left hand. The Renaissance interpretation of the figure suggests the possibility that these attributes were part of an ancient transformation of the river god into another divinity. On the other hand, the reported presence of a crown is confirmed by a sharp depression on the back of the head indicating that some such attribute may have been part of the original conception of the figure. Unfortunately, the badly-worn Pandosia stater gives no hint as to whether the archetype wore such a crown. Even granting that the vine recorded above was a stylized support for the lights of a *lychnophoros*, it could easily have been part of a copyist's adaptation of a famous statue to serve a new purpose. Conceivably, such an adaptation might have been made even in the fifth century. For, though no comparable *lychnophoroi* are known from that century, the idea of such a figure is at least as old as Homer.[36] Even if such a figure was a purely literary creation in Homer, at any later time it might have been translated into plastic reality. This explanation would have the added merit of providing a classical precedent for the popularity of this type in the first century B.C.[37] In any case, the essential adaptability of the *offerente* to this purpose is undeniable. Which of these alternatives is the true one cannot be said. One indisputable fact remains: no one devising a figure for the express purpose of a *lychnophoros* would invent the Idolino type, because nothing could be less convenient for that end than its open right palm. Whenever it was made and whatever its final transformation, such a type must always have been primarily an *offerente* and secondarily a *lychnophoros*; that is, a *lychnophoros* of this type must have been derived from a statuary type originating for quite another purpose.[38]

Hence the iconographic and stylistic characteristics of the Idolino and their marked parallelism with the Pandosia stater can best be explained by the assumption that both statue and coin type reproduce a lost statue of the river god Krathis whose waters were famed in antiquity for their magical powers.[39] That this statue was made about 430 B.C. by an artist influenced by contemporary Polykleitan works is undeniable. The highly personal nature of his style remains.[40] It is equally clear that he must have taken over the iconographic type of his statue from the famous earlier statuary type in Selinus.[41] This procedure is by no

36. *Odyssey*, VII, 100 ff. Cf. Lucretius, *De rerum natura*, II, 24 ff.
37. The use of the bronze statuette discussed on p. 22, note 38, is of considerable interest in this connection. Although described as a support for στλεγγίδες it is more likely a candelabrum, since there is no way of determining that the now broken side extensions would have been too small to support candles, if not lamps. If, in the fourth century, such a statuette stood on top of a candelabrum, the way to the later use of the type itself as a *lychnophoros* was already prepared, since the earlier candelabrum and the later *lychnophoros* belonged to a similar sphere.
38. The Roman base on which the figure stood, generally interpreted as the addition of a late antique connoisseur on its arrival from Greece, is as necessary an addition to a statue plundered from Southern Italy.

39. Of healing and bleaching the hair of human beings golden, of cattle, white. Cf. Euripides, *Troiades*, 224–229; Ovid, *Metamorphoses*, XV, 315; Pliny, *Historia Naturalis*, XXXI, 10; Strabo, VI, 1, 13, X, 1, 14.
40. It is interesting to recall that Lange, *op. cit.*, pp. 217 ff., who regarded the Idolino as a good copy of a Polykleitan statue suggested that its execution might be "italisch," while Schwabacher, "Die Tetradrachmenprägung von Selinunt," p. 82, remarked on the analogy between the Idolino and the later Selinuntine dies.
41. The long-noted similarity between the Idolino and the well-known Polykleitan bronze statuette in the Louvre (A. de Ridder, *Bronzes antiques du Louvre*, Paris, I, 1913, No. 183, pl. 19) is an instructive case to notice at this point. Iconographically, the figures are closely related. Stylistically, too, they share a few characteristics. But the basic type and style of the sturdy, heavy-set Louvre figure are thoroughly Polykleitan, and utterly different from the angular grace, the lighter, more delicate character of the Idolino. It seems reasonable to assume that in this Louvre statuette we have a purely Polykleitan version of the iconographic type developing out of the transitional period in such a figure as the youth from Agrigento, and leading to the Selinus types, a popular iconographic type which spread to other regions, too. A bronze statuette in Athens (V. Stais, *Marbres et bronzes du Musée National*, Athens, 1910, I, pp. 318–319, No. 7402) is a further example of the widespread adoption of this iconographic type.
Totally different is the case of the previously discovered Pompeii statue (see J. Sieveking, in Br.-Br., Nos. 736, 737, for discussion and extensive bibliography) which is clearly the product of a neoclassical sculptor familiar not only with this iconographic type but, in all probability, with these very works, on whose basis he has modelled his hybrid creation. As Sieveking rightly pointed out, therefore, this statue depends on earlier prototypes in Italy and, from the beginning, was probably created as a *lychnophoros*.
Finally, it is well to observe that a marble statue of a youth in the Metropolitan Museum (G. M. A. Richter, *Bulletin of the Metropolitan Museum of Art*, XXI, 1926, pp. 255 ff., and fig. 2) is not related to the Selinus-Pandosia group either typologically or stylistically. Particularly when seen from the side, it is clear that the left leg came forward, preceding the right, thereby removing it from the type under consideration. Furthermore, its subtle wealth of inherent vitality is certainly Attic. This case affords a vivid illustration of the tremendous importance of seemingly slight differences in a period which took for granted a rare degree of refinement and perception in the spectator. The Metropolitan figure has been considered a copy of a Greek original also reflected in a slightly earlier marble statuette in Berlin (*op. cit.*, and Carl Blümel, *Katalog der Sammlung antiker Skulpturen*, Berlin,

means curious, especially when it is recalled that the Selinus didrachm was so popular and highly regarded as to be almost literally copied on the coinage of Solus.[42] Given the need of making a comparable statue of a river god, such a nearby precedent would not have been overlooked, nor would the example of its application to numismatic usage, as several other coins of the region testify.[43]

This lost statue of the river god Krathis is reflected in still another piece, a bronze statuette in the Metropolitan Museum[44] (Pl. v, Fig. 12). For, although it presents certain variations, notably in the different style of coiffure and the more usual position of the left leg, this statuette belongs to the Krathis type in both iconography and style. The open right palm and the angle of the left hand demand the same attributes. Again, the familiar slender, flat forms, the long, angular lines of the body, its silhouette, its V-shaped pelvis, its unobtrusive modelling of the torso in order not to disturb the angular verticality of effect by competing horizontals unite this statuette to both the Pandosia stater and the Idolino. On the basis of these characteristics, it may be considered of contemporary South Italian workmanship.[45]

Inasmuch as the Hypsas didrachm of Selinus and the Krathis stater of Pandosia are types that do not occur on the coinage of any other region of the ancient world, the most reasonable explanation for the existence of such a group of iconographically and stylistically related statues and statuettes as has just been discussed is that these coin types are not to be regarded as purely or primarily numismatic creations but as fine and faithful reproductions of contemporary statues. That these lost statues were of local South Italian or Sicilian workmanship is equally clear. By virtue of the relationship which the Pompeii youth, the Idolino, and the Somzée, Bibliothèque Nationale, Budapest, and Metropolitan statuettes bear to these coin types and, hence, to their archetypes, they, too, may be regarded as South Italian or Sicilian works.[46] Indeed, wherever the provenance of one of these figures is known, it is Italian.[47]

1931, IV, K 140, pl. 24). The angularity of the shoulders, the flatness of the contour of the body, the smoothness of the modelling, a certain artificiality of pose and expression suggest, rather, that the Berlin statuette is a neo-classical work deriving possibly from the original of the Metropolitan figure.

42. Cf. G. F. Hill, *Coins of Ancient Sicily*, London, 1903, pl. VI, No. 14, and p. 95, who assumed that the chance resemblance of ΣΟΛΟΝΤΙΝΟΝ to ΣΕΛΙΝΟΝΤΙΟΝ prompted this plagiarism in an attempt on the part of Solus to gain acceptance for its coinage. Panormus, too, adapted Selinuntine types for one of its tetradrachms. See E. Gabrici, "Notes on Sicilian Numismatics," *Num. Chr.*, ser. v, vol. XI, 1931, p. 78, No. 1; p. 80 f., pl. VI, No. 1.

43. Cf., for example, the preceding discussion of the litrae of Leontini and Stiela. W. Schwabacher, too, has described the Stiela and Leontini types as stemming from the Hypsas didrachm ("Die Tetradrachmenprägung von Selinunt," p. 75).

Schwabacher ("Some Coins of Metapontum in the Royal Collection at Copenhagen," *Acta Archaeologica*, x, 1939, p. 124, figs. 1, 2) has recently published a rare fifth-century coin of Metapontum which he describes as a river god probably holding a patera in his right hand, a reed in his left. Although the damaged state of the piece precludes any final statement, it seems likely that the reverse reproduces the statue of a river god and therefore stands in much the same relation to the Hypsas didrachm as does the Pandosia stater. It is far too unlike the famous Acheloos type of Metapontum to be characterized in Schwabacher's words as an "annex" to it.

For a list of coin types of this region which represent river gods, see S. Mirone, "Les divinités fluviales représentées sur les monnaies antiques de la Sicile," *R. N.*, ser. IV, vol. XXI, 1917, pp. 17–18 ff., and "Les divinités fluviales sur les monnaies antiques de la Grande-Grèce," *R. N.*, ser. IV, vol. XXX, 1927, pp. 127 ff.

44. No. 12.235.1 Ht: 14.1 cm. Cast solid. Right foot and tips of right fingers missing. Part of tang preserved on left foot. Hole at top of head. No provenance indicated. Dated by G. M. A. Richter, *Greek, Etruscan and Roman Bronzes*, New York, 1915, p. 58, No. 88, in the second half of the fifth century B.C. and described as Polykleitan. See addendum, p. 66.

45. Furtwängler, *Masterpieces*, p. 287, mentioned a marble statue in the Palazzo Barberini (F. Matz and F. von Duhn, *Antike Bildwerke in Rom*, Leipzig, 1881, I, p. 327, No. 1111) which he considered so close to the Idolino as possibly to be a copy of it. Inasmuch as the head does not belong to the body (see *Einzelaufnahmen*, No. 2886), and the stance is utterly unlike that of the Idolino, the statue cannot be considered specifically related. However, it is conceivable that the Barberini statue reflects an original of the same artistic circle, as Furtwängler suggested.

A possible local variant of the type is to be found in a small unpublished bronze statuette from the Astuto Collection, of very inferior workmanship, in the Museo Nazionale in Palermo, tagged 56 and marked 56 and 21.

46. With the already noted exception of the Budapest statuette, all the figures discussed above and interpreted as river gods show a characteristic lack of pubic hair—a welcome iconographic proof of the relationships established here.

47. After the preparation of this discussion, it is gratifying to find that Picard (*Manuel d'archéologie grecque*, II¹, pp. 270–271, on stylistic grounds, considers the Idolino an Italian bronze made under Greek influence, and a fifth-century original. He goes so far as to say "les dieux-fleuves des monnaies de Sélinonte, Sélinous ou Hypsas, l'évoqueraient aussi"!

IV

IN THE latter part of the fifth century B.C., Segesta struck tetradrachms representing the river god Krimisos.[1] The youthful divinity appears as a hunter wearing a pilos pushed back on his neck, with a chlamys cast over his arm, a baldric slung over his right shoulder, and endromides on his feet (Pl. VI, Fig. 1). His raised left leg rests upon a rock and supports his left arm, while his right hand leans nonchalantly on his hip. He faces right, grasps two spears in his left hand, and is accompanied by two hounds. The highly plastic quality of this beautiful type together with the knowledge that the Krimisos was worshipped in human form at Segesta,[2] has evoked the opinion that the tetradrachm reproduces a bronze statue.[3] Although no exact statuary replica of the type exists, three related monuments attest the validity of this suggestion.

Strikingly similar to the Segesta tetradrachm is the representation of a young hunter on a black-figured Campanian lekythos from Paestum[4] (Pl. VI, Fig. 2). All the essential characteristics of the coin type are repeated in reverse: the raised leg, the hand on the hip, the pilos, chlamys, and boots, even the baldric. Most important of all, this representation is clearly dependent upon a statue, for the vase painter has gone so far as to reproduce the base on which the statue stood.[5] Indeed, given the analogy between the two figures, it is tempting to consider that in representing the heroized dead, the vase painter used a statue exactly like the Krimisos as his model, modifying it enough to allow the deceased to receive an offering, hence shifting his spear and catching it by the thumb of the hand resting on the hip. Certainly, such a figure of a young hunter-god lent itself remarkably well to this adaptation. Whether that model actually was the Krimisos cannot be said. The fact remains that on this lekythos, dated in the third quarter of the fourth century B.C.,[6] a statue very

1. Obv: [Σ]ΕΓΕΣΤΑΙΩΝ. As described in text. Pl. VI, Fig. 1 from Grose, pl. LXXXVII, No. 7. Rev: ΣΕΓΕΣΤΑΖΙΑ. Head of Segesta; or Segesta standing, crowned by Victory, and holding branch and patera over altar; or quadriga, charioteer being crowned by Victory (for these variations see Jean Babelon, *Catalogue de la collection de Luynes*, Paris, 1924, I, Nos. 1120–1122).

Originally dated 461–415 B.C., the type was restricted to 416–413 by A. J. Evans (*Syracusan Medallions*, London, 1892, pp. 90 ff.) on the grounds that it was part of the "show coinage" designed to impress contemporary Athenians in a campaign to secure Athenian coöperation against Selinus and Syracuse. Later dated 415–409 B.C. by Grose, p. 302 and Head, *H. N.*, p. 164. However, P. Lederer, *Die Tetradrachmenprägung von Segesta*, Munich, 1910, pp. 28 ff., on the basis of his study of the 11 known dies and their 47 examples, considered that the type was inaugurated about the middle of the century. Stating that the epigraphical evidence provided by these coins is inconsistent and cannot serve as the basis for a chronological system, he distributed the early dies at five to ten year intervals arbitrarily beginning with the Athenian treaty of 454/3. Thus dies 1–3 occupy the period 454–30; die 4 is dated about 426, leaving 19 years for the remaining seven dies— not a very convincing distribution. Hence, the precise date at which this type was introduced remains unsettled, and can probably only be determined on stylistic grounds.

2. Aelian, *Varia Historia*, II, 33. For additional references to the Krimisos see the article by Ziegler in *R. E.*, XI, col. 1859.

Although the dies vary in several respects—the number of dogs, the angle of the figure and so forth—the figure itself is generally constant in all the details described above. However, on one die (Lederer's No. 4), the representation of the god differs in several details, chief among them being the absence of the pilos and the presence of a horn springing from the front of the head. Lederer (*op. cit.*, pp. 45 ff.) rejected the generally accepted interpretation of the normal pilos type as the river god Krimisos whose union with the nymph Egesta, a union which he effected in the form of a dog, resulted in the birth of Egestos, the hero-founder. He preferred to interpret the normal type as that hero-founder, Egestos, and the unique die, because of the presence of the horn, as the river god Krimisos. This interpretation was later accepted by both Matz (*Die Naturpersonificationen in der griechischen Kunst*, p. 103) and Imhoof-Blumer (*Fluss- und Meergötter auf griechischen und römischen Münzen*, Geneva, 1924, p. 43, No. 85).

Whatever the motivation of this unique die may have been, it is hardly possible that anyone, including a fifth-century Greek, could be expected to interpret two such essentially similar and contemporary numismatic types as representations of two different gods simply because they differ in certain lesser details. Whoever the god may be, it is one god and not two that must be explained; that is, the unique die is certainly a variant of the major type. Hence the presence on this one figure of a horn, the common attribute of river gods, is of importance for the entire series, and suggests the greater probability of the old explanation of the whole group as illustrative of the Krimisos—an explanation retained in the present discussion. It is more than likely that the statue these numismatic types probably reflect was characterized by the horn present on one die. Indeed, it is altogether possible that the statue showed the river god actually wearing a pilos on his head and that, on the great majority of dies, the pilos was pushed back on the neck to achieve a more successful composition for the circular space while, in one instance, it was entirely omitted in order to render the horns more clearly visible.

3. A. Salinas, *Sul tipo de' tetradrammi di Segesta*, Florence, 1870, p. 14.

4. Now in Braunschweig. *Corpus Vasorum Antiquorum*, XII, 4 (*Deutschland*, IV, *Braunschweig*, by A. Greifenhagen), Munich, 1940, pl. XXXIV.

5. Greifenhagen, *loc. cit.*, describes the figure as a warrior standing on an altar. I think the illustration speaks for itself.

6. *Ibid.*

FIG. 1. Cambridge, Fitzwilliam Museum: Obverse of Tetradrachm of Segesta

FIG. 3. Naples, Museo Nazionale: Bronze Statuette from Herculaneum

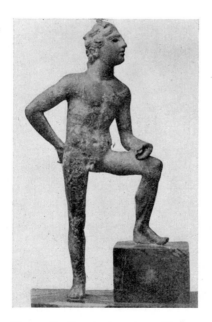

FIG. 4. Berlin, Antiquarium: Bronze Statuette

FIG. 2. Braunschweig, Herzog Anton Ulrich-Museum: Detail of a Campanian Lekythos from Paestum

PLATE VI

APOLLO AT METAPONTUM

I

THERE IS every reason to believe that the statue of Apollo which Herodotus saw surrounded by laurels in the marketplace at Metapontum[1] was reproduced on that city's coinage throughout the greater part of the fifth century B.C. Prominent among Metapontine staters is the series bearing as its reverse type a nude figure of Apollo who stands looking toward right, holding a laurel branch in his right hand and a bow in his left[2] (Pl. VII, Fig. 1). Although the type varies from die to die, especially in the rendering of the laurel, the angle at which the attributes are held and, in one instance, in the presence of an altar, such minor variations are obviously modifications of the individual die-cutter, the basic type remaining static.[3] Inasmuch as this is the sole figure of Apollo with a laurel branch among the coin types of Metapontum, it seems safe to conclude that this stater represents the statue seen by Herodotus,[4] as other writers have agreed. Certainly, the type itself gives every indication of reproducing a statue set up during the decade 470–460, and com-

memorated immediately thereafter on the city's coinage.

Two works of sculpture lend support to this contention. The first, a small bronze statuette in the British Museum[5] (Pl. VII, Fig. 2), is strikingly similar to the coin in both type and style. A comparison of Figs. 1 and 2 shows that the figures are alike in attitude and stance as well as in such an iconographic detail as the coiffure. Furthermore, it reveals a uniformity of style between coin type and statuette that extends to the smallest details: from the conspicuous eyes, long nose, and lean jaws of the face to the modelling of the torso—from the placing of the pectoral muscles to the shape of the pelvis—and including the entire silhouette of the angular, provincial figure. Only in the precise angle of the extended right arm does the statuette differ slightly from the coin type. However, this minor difference in no way alters the essential fact that the statuette appears to be a contemporary replica of the lost statue seen by Herodotus in the agora of Metapontum. As such, the little figure is of particular interest, and should be restored with the laurel branch and bow of the stater, attributes already indicated by the very nature and position of the hands.[6]

The second reflection of the Metapontine archetype, also in the British Museum, is a life-size bronze statue found in Egypt at Zifteh[7] (Pl. VII, Fig. 3). Iconographically, this statue is identical with the coin type, standing on the right foot,

1. IV, 15: καὶ νῦν ἔστηκε ἀνδριὰς ἐπωνυμίην ἔχων Ἀριστέω παρ' αὐτῷ τῷ ἀγάλματι τοῦ Ἀπόλλωνος· πέριξ δὲ αὐτὸν δάφναι ἑστᾶσι· τὸ δὲ ἄγαλμα ἐν τῇ ἀγορῇ ἵδρυται·
2. Obv: META Ear of barley; occasionally, a grasshopper in the right field. See, S. P. Noe, *The Coinage of Metapontum,* Part II (*Numismatic Notes and Monographs,* No. 47), New York, 1931, pl. XXIV, Nos. 314–319, pp. 8, 61 ff. Usually dated 470–400 B.C.; according to Mr. Noe, certainly belonging to the period *ca* 470. Pl. VII, Fig. 1 from Hill, *Select Greek Coins,* pl. XXXIX, 4.
3. S. Mirone ("Copies de statues sur les monnaies de la Grande Grèce," *R.N.,* ser. IV, vol. XXVII, 1924, pp. 10 ff.), accepting the statue seen by Herodotus as represented on the type shown here in Fig. 1, differentiated the variant having an altar and considered it to be a different figure—a statue of Aristeas. Given the degree of similarity between the variants alone, such an idea is unthinkable. For Mirone's additional comments on this coin see below, p. 39, note 12.
4. Head, *H.N.,* p. 76, said that the figure on the coin was "probably suggested by" the statue Herodotus mentions. F. Lenormant, *La Grande-Grèce,* Paris, I, 1881, p. 127 went so far as to declare that the monument described by Herodotus was reproduced on the coinage of Metapontum toward the middle of the fifth century. So, too, Mayer, in his article *Metapontum* in *R.E.,* XV, col. 1361, referred to the figure as "ein statuarischer Typus." Mr. Noe has called my attention to a passage in J. Overbeck, *Griechische Kunstmythologie,* Leipzig, 1889, III, pp. 77–78, where the author, apparently not remembering Herodotus' statement, doubted the likelihood that the coin reflects a statuary type.

5. No. 677. Ht: 5⅛". Eyes hollow; right hand, left foot, injured. Formerly in the Blacas Collection. Provenance not indicated. H. B. Walters, *Catalogue of the Bronzes, Greek, Roman, and Etruscan, in the British Museum,* p. 112.
6. Described by V. H. Poulsen, "Der strenge Stil," p. 102 and fig. 69 as related to Selinuntine sculpture and, probably for this reason, as West Sicilian in style.
7. No. 828. Ht: 1.57 m. (5' 3"). Whites of eyes of silver; iris originally inlaid; nipples copper; hair worked separately and attached. Cast in nine pieces. Feet and base restored. Formerly in the collection of M. Mimaut, French Consul General in Egypt, and acquired by the British Museum in 1840. Walters, *op. cit.,* p. 150; *idem, Select Bronzes,* London, 1915, Pl. XLI; *Description of the Collection of Ancient Marbles in the British Museum,* London, XI, 1861, pl. XXXIII (here part of the right and the lower part of the left leg are described as restored, too); Adolf Michaelis, *An-*

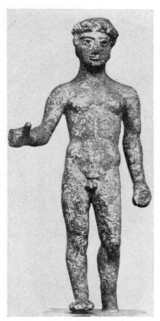

FIG. 2. London, British Museum: Bronze Statuette

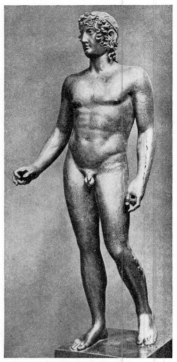

FIG. 3. London, British Museum: Bronze Statue Found in Egypt

FIG. 1. London, British Museum: Reverse of Stater of Metapontum

PLATE VII

with the left leg drawn back and to the side, and having arms that hang in comparable positions and are equipped with bars to help support the attributes. This typological relationship is so close as to make probable the restoration of a laurel branch to the right hand and of a bow to the left.[8] The broad, rather angular shoulders, the outline of the torso, and the general proportions of both statue and coin type are very similar. Here, however, the resemblance ceases. For the flabbiness of

the modelling as well as the type and rendering of the head proclaim the neo-classical origin of the work. Therefore, in view of its analogies to the stater, it is reasonable to consider the British Museum statue a first century B.C. neo-classical reflection of the lost Metapontine statue.[9] This statue, it will be recalled, is the one sculpture reproduced on the coinage of Magna Graecia and Sicily from 480 to 323 B.C. for which there is both documentary and monumental evidence.

II

THE ORGANIC development of a statuary type until its entire range of potential nuances of movement and posture has been explored, that basic concept of Greek sculpture so extensively illustrated in the evolution of the *kouros*, may be seen on a more restricted scale behind the Apollo on the reverse of the fifth-century half-stater of Metapontum[1] (Pl. VIII, Fig. 1). The youthful, beardless god stands facing, resting lightly on his right leg, as he turns his head sharply toward his left; his

right hand leans on his hip; his left grasps a strung bow. That this numismatic type reproduces a statue is evident from consideration of a group of bronze statuettes which form a sequence running from shortly after the middle of the fifth to the latter part of the fourth century B.C.

Plate VIII, Figs. 2 and 3 illustrate the earliest members of this group, the former in the Berlin Münz-Kabinett,[2] the latter last known at the sale of the Pozzi Collection in 1919.[3] Despite the slight typological and stylistic advance represented by the former Pozzi figure over the Berlin bronze, a development apparent in the inclination of the head, the position of the left leg, and the greater looseness and elongation of the body, the statu-

---

cient Marbles in Great Britain, Cambridge, 1882, p. 167 and "Statua di Bacco trovata nella Villa Adriana," *Annali*, LV, 1883, p. 141; F. de Clarac, *Musée de sculpture*, III, No. 929B, pl. 482C. Furtwängler, *Masterpieces*, p. 353 and fig. 151, considered the statue a Hellenistic imitation of a work by Euphranor and associated it with the former Sabouroff and Gréau bronzes in Berlin, an opinion that is not acceptable. (Cf. *Führer durch des Antiquarium*, No. Sk. I and No. 7934, pls. 39, 73.) Walters dated the piece in the first century B.C., and described it as Hellenistic with traces of Egyptian influence, a characterization with which it is scarcely possible to agree! H. Bulle, *Der schöne Mensch im Altertum*, col. 155, pl. LXXXI, recognized the classicistic character of the statue and dated it in the first century B.C.

8. Both Furtwängler and Walters suggested the restoration of a laurel branch to the right hand on purely theoretical and formal grounds. Furtwängular insisted that the bars in the left hand were simply to fasten the fingers together securely, and not the traces of an attribute. However, as Michaelis implied in his description of the bars, they probably indicate the presence of an attribute in the left hand, too. For, as Karl Lehmann assures me, there is no technical reason for the presence of such bars as supports in a bronze statue, whereas they have a certain value in holding an attribute in place.

9. Note, too, a carnelian engraved with a representation of Apollo differing from the Metapontum type only in the direction of the head, in this case, turned toward the figure's left (Adolf Furtwängler, *Die antiken Gemmen*, Leipzig and Berlin, 1900, p. 52, No. 38, pl. X). In all probability, the gem reflects a statue, and it is entirely possible that either it or its statuary prototype may be a variant of the Metapontum archetype.

1. Obv: META to right, downward. Ear of barley. Reverse type within laurel wreath. Wt: 3.66 gr. Grose, p. 122, pl. XXXII, 9, here Fig. 1B. Accepted by Grose (*ibid.*, and in "Some Rare Coins of Magna Graecia," *Num. Chr.*, ser. IV, vol. XVI, 1916, pp. 211–

212, pl. VII, 5) as following 470, on grounds of style and epigraphy; by A. Sambon ("Metaponte sous le jong des Lucaniens," *R.N.*, ser. IV, vol. XIX, 1915, p. 97) as toward 450–430 and, like Rhegion and Terina, bearing an olive crown in token of the oil trade with those cities. In opposition to this opinion, Head (*H.N.*, p. 78) maintained that the unique occurrence of the half-stater in a coinage at the time divided into thirds and sixths indicated that the coin should be dated 350–330 and the coinage assimilated to that of Thurium. The earlier date is accepted by Noe in his discussion of No. 320, *The Coinage of Metapontum*, Part II. W. Schwabacher, "Die Tetradrachmenprägung von Selinunt," p. 74, dated this type near the beginning of his second Selinuntine group of 445–435 B.C.

2. Inv. No. 30894. Ht: 9.4 cm. Left hand, both feet and ankles lacking. Upper surface covered with grainy, dark patina flecked with small, grass-green spots. Cast solid. Originally in the Dressel Collection; bequeathed to the coin cabinet in 1922 (K. A. Neugebauer, "Erwerbungen der Antiker-Sammlungen in Deutschland. Berlin," *A.A.*, 1922, cols. 92 ff., No. 43, fig. 43; reproduced by Reinach, *Répertoire*, VI, p. 135, No. 4).

3. A. Sambon ("L'Exposition d'art antique au Petit Palais," *Le Musée*, II, 1905, p. 181, fig. 17, and S. Reinach, *R.A.*, ser. V, vol. X, 1919, p. 231. Reproduced by Reinach, *Répertoire*, in both IV, p. 345, No. 6 and V, p. 290, No. 6, the latter being identical with the *R.A.* illustration. No description or indication of the provenance given in any reference; simply characterized by Sambon, *loc. cit.*, as fifth century. Present location unknown to me.

FIG. 2. Berlin, Münz-Kabinett: Bronze Statuette

FIG. 3. Former Pozzi Collection: Bronze Statuette

FIG. 1A. New York, American Numismatic Society: Reverse of Half-Stater of Metapontum

FIG. 1B. Cambridge, Fitzwilliam Museum: Reverse of Half-Stater of Metapontum

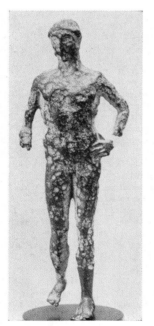

FIG. 4. New York, Metropolitan Museum of Art: Bronze Statuette from Cyprus

FIG. 5. Hannover, Kestner-Museum: Bronze Statuette

PLATE VIII

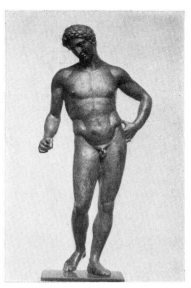

Fig. 6. Madrid, Museo Arqueológico Nacional: Bronze Statuette from Mallorca

Fig. 7. Karlsruhe, Badisches Landesmuseum: Bronze Statuette Found near Mechtersheim

Fig. 8. Bonn, Provinzialmuseum: Bronze Statuette

ettes are so closely interrelated as to probably constitute small copies of a monumental statue made about 450 B.C. Very likely, that statue is faithfully reflected in the still rather solid, quiet forms of the Berlin figure and in the slight turn of his large-eyed, sombre face. A decade would suffice to account for the differences between the statuettes. The essential similarity of the modelling of the V-shaped torsos and the short-haired, filleted heads, is not concealed by the differences between the figures or by the more expressive face of the former Pozzi bronze.[4]

A glance at the Metapontum half-stater clarifies the restoration of the figures, for they are so close to the coin as to ensure the correctness of introducing a bow into the hole in the former Pozzi figure's bent left hand, and of reconstructing an identical hand and bow for the Berlin statuette. Indeed, the analogy between the slender, rather angular Apollo of the coin type and the former Pozzi bronze, especially the identity of their sil-

houettes, is striking and suggests a date of about 440 for the half-stater.[5] One major difference separates the coin type from these statuettes: the direction in which the head is turned and, with it, the line of the shoulders. On this score, too, the remaining figures of the group are of particular interest.

For these remaining statuettes, one in the Metropolitan Museum in New York[6] (Pl. VIII, Fig. 4), one in the Kestner Museum in Hannover[7] (Pl. VIII, Fig. 5), another in the Museo Arqueológico Nacional in Madrid[8] (Fig. 6), and two statuettes

4. Neugebauer, *loc. cit.*, also noted the similarity of the Berlin and Pozzi statuettes, considering the latter to be the nearest known figure to the former in motif. However, he thought the Pozzi figure Greek, and the Berlin statuette, because of its plump proportions, an Etruscan work closely connected with Greek prototypes. Although it is impossible to be absolutely positive on the basis of this one photograph, such an attribution seems unwarranted. See text for further discussion of this point.

5. A date based on the comparative evidence of sculpture which accords very well with Schwabacher's numismatic date cited in note 1.

6. Acc. No. C.B.338. Ht: 10.2 cm. Right hand and wrist, piece of left forearm, forepart of right foot missing. Green patina partly removed. Cast solid. Nipples separately inserted. Badly corroded. Considered to be fourth-century work. From Curium. G. M. A. Richter, *Greek, Etruscan and Roman Bronzes*, New York, 1915, pp. 64–65, No. 105; L. P. di Cesnola, *A Descriptive Atlas of the Cesnola Collection of Cypriote Antiquities in the Metropolitan Museum of Art, New York*, New York, 1903, III, pl. LXVI, 1; J. L. Myres, *Handbook of the Cesnola Collection of Antiquities from Cyprus*, New York, 1914, p. 499, No. 5027; Reinach, *Répertoire*, v, p. 291, No. 4, and Cesnola, *loc. cit.*, illustrate the figure in reverse.

7. Briefly noted by C. Küthmann, *A.A.*, 1928, cols. 692–693, figs. 15–16. Dimensions not indicated. Broken fragment of former attribute in right hand.

8. Ht: 24.5 cm. Excavated in Alcudia, Mallorca, in 1928. Gerhart Rodenwaldt, *Arte clásico*, Barcelona, 1933, 2nd ed., p. 784, No. 2

dependent upon a common archetype, one in Karlsruhe[9] (Fig. 7), and one in Bonn[10] (Fig. 8), are alike in being exact typological reversals of the

half-stater type. Like the coin type, they represent the head turned toward the side of the extended arm and relaxed leg, with a corresponding slight lowering of one shoulder. The New York and Hannover figures are closest to the fifth-century statuettes in one detail: they, alone, show the hand as clasping the hip rather than resting upon it. Even in its present badly preserved state, the marked similarities of the New York figure to the Hannover statuette are apparent, especially in such details as the simplified coiffure, the shape of the eyes, and the modelling of the abdomen. Like the Berlin and Pozzi statuettes, they may well reflect a common archetype, in this case, a fourth-century development of the type.[11] Behind the intimately related Madrid, Karlsruhe, and Bonn figures must lie a common mid-fourth-century archetype that is very likely most faithfully reflected in the heavier, more contained, Madrid statuette. For an intermediate manneristic statue must stand between the mid-fourth-century archetype and its Roman replicas in Karlsruhe and Bonn.

However one may choose to interpret the rela-

and p. 880; A. Garcia y Bellido, "Archaeologische Ausgrabungen und Forschungen in Spanien von 1930 bis 1940," *A.A.*, 1941, p. 204, fig. 8.

9. Ht: 23 cm. Attribute, little finger of right hand, and left nipple, missing. Found in 1837 near Mechtersheim near Speier. Karl Schumacher, *Beschreibung der Sammlung antiker Bronzen*, Karlsruhe, 1890, p. 231 and pl. XXVII. Furtwängler, *Masterpieces*, p. 300, fig. 128 described the piece as Roman, probably made in Gaul, with a ring on the left little finger. He thought it reflected a fourth-century original by Skopas, citing a mingling of Polykleitan influence in the body and stance with a grace of movement and Attic details such as the hair—a combination, in any case, as easily fourth-century South Italian as Scopaic. He accepted the theory that the statuette, together with a coin of Marcus Aurelius, reproduced a youthful Asklepios leaning on a staff. However, this coin (W. Wroth, "Apollo with the Aesculapian Staff," *Num. Chr.*, ser. III, vol. II, 1882, pl. XIV, No. 3, pp. 301–305), whether it represents Apollo with Asklepios' staff, as Wroth maintained, or a youthful Asklepios, as Wieseler held ("Die bildlichen Darstellungen des jugendlichen und unbärtigen Aesculap," *Göttinger Nachrichten*, 1888, pp. 152 ff.), shows a different statuary type having nothing to do with the Karlsruhe figure, as its long, flowing hair, different stance, and left hand with its side against the hip indicate. A. von Sallet ("Beiträge zur antiken Münz- und Alterthumskunde," *Z.f.N.*, IX, 1882, pp. 139–141) considered the Karlsruhe statuette and a second figure in Bonn (see note 10) to be Apollo or Asklepios and, on the basis of the Aurelian coin, restored a snake staff to both figures. K. A. Neugebauer ("Bronzestatuette des Narkissos von Mechtersheim," *Siebenundachtzigstes Winckelmannsprogramm*, Berlin, 1927), recognizing the fallacy of the Asklepios theory, restored the Karlsruhe figure with a javelin and explained it as a Narkissos. The awkward overlapping of the right arm and javelin necessitated by this suggestion (see his fig. 5) produces an unsatisfactory effect, while the ponderation of the figure does not require a tall support. Given the analogy between this figure in Karlsruhe, the Metapontum coin, and the Berlin and former Pozzi statuettes, it is more convincing to interpret it, too, as a representation of Apollo grasping a bow in his right hand. Certainly, the Karlsruhe statuette is closer to the above-mentioned works than to any of the other types with which it has been associated. Described by Neugebauer as a classicistic work of the imperial period. The Karlsruhe statuette is also quoted in Friederichs-Wolters, *Die Gipsabgüsse antiker Bildwerke*, Berlin, 1885, No. 1758 and illustrated in *Germania Romana*, Bamberg, 1922, pl. LXXII, 3, p. xx, *Germania Romana*, IV, Bamberg, 1928, pl. XXXIX, 1 and p. 61, and Reinach, *Répertoire*, II, p. 102, No. 3. For the complete bibliography, see Neugebauer, *op. cit.*, p. 3, note 3. The discussion of this statuette by F. von Duhn, *Verzeichnis der Abgüsse der Universität Heidelberg*, 1887, No. 176 is not available to me.

10. Ht: 27.5 cm. Ring finger of left hand, three first toes of left foot, most of attribute of right hand missing. Left arm, leg, forepart of left foot broken and rejoined; shin and thigh of right leg, forepart of foot and heel separated. Put together and restored. Almost entire lower half of right glutaeus restored in tin; other areas, in copper. Held by iron rivets. Originally cast solid. Provenance unknown. Entered the Bonn collection in 1823 from the collection of Prince Isenberg, the latter apparently largely assembled in Italy. For a lengthy technical analysis of the figure see Overbeck, "Bronzestatuetten im kgl. rheinischen Museum vaterländischer Alterthümer," *Jahrbücher des Vereins von Al-*

terthumsfreunden im Rheinlande, XVII, 1851, pp. 61–69, pl. 1, and Neugebauer, "Bronzestatuette des Narkissos," pp. 19 ff. Also published by Hans Lehner, *Führer durch das Provinzialmuseum in Bonn*, I, Bonn, 1915, pp. 59 ff., pl. XIV, 1, and quoted by Friederichs-Wolters, *loc. cit.*, and reproduced by Reinach, *Répertoire*, II, p. 550, No. 1 and in *Germania Romana*, Bamberg, 1922, pl. LXXIV, 2 and p. xx. For reference to former doubt in regard to the authenticity of the statuette see Urlichs, "Zur Kritik und Erklärung," *Jahrbücher des Vereins von Alterthumsfreunden im Rheinlande*, XXV, 1857, p. 26, No. 6. Overbeck, *loc. cit.*, interpreted the figure as an athlete holding a strigil, an opinion tentatively repeated by Lehner, *loc. cit.*; generally considered a replica of the Karlsruhe statuette, hence sometimes explained as Apollo or Asklepios (von Sallet, Friederichs-Wolters, *loc. cit.*). Neugebauer, *loc. cit.*, acknowledging the bad quality of the repairs made to the Bonn statuette, still thought that differences between the Bonn and Karlsruhe figures—the angle of the left arm, the position of the left hand, etc.—were sufficient to establish the Bonn figure as a different iconographic type, a type that he explained as Hermes carrying a purse. Again, this interpretation is not convincing. If, as Neugebauer insisted, the knobby remains of an attribute in the right hand are not the result of later filing or wear, but the original tip of the missing attribute, it is altogether possible that the figure held a bow by its tip—its curving shape would balance the figure well. In any case, once the errors resulting from mistaken restorations are substracted, the Bonn and Karlsruhe figures are so alike that they undoubtedly reflect a common archetype.

11. Küthmann, who remarked on the analogy of these two statuettes, *loc. cit.*, nonetheless dated the Kestner figure not later than 400, especially because of the treatment of the eyes. The scale and provincial workmanship of the statuette as well as the obvious simplification of the head account for this *retardataire* detail.

tionship of this series of statues and their small replicas, certain conclusions result from the previous considerations. Clearly, these statuettes represent progressive stages in the evolution of a statuary type characterized primarily as a youthful Apollo standing with his weight on one leg, the other being placed lightly to the side, with one hand resting on the hip of the supporting leg, and the other holding a bow. Midway between what might be called the fifth- and the fourth-century versions of this type stands the Apollo of the Metapontum half-stater, closest to the fifth-century type, yet sharing the feature of the turned head with the fourth-century group. Inasmuch as it is highly improbable that such an organic development would proceed from sculpture to numismatics to sculpture, it is reasonable to assume that the half-stater type reflects a step in this development which is otherwise lost; in other words, that the Metapontine half-stater type reproduces a lost statue of Apollo which stood in Metapontum and was reproduced on the city's coinage.[12] Finally, since this step in the typological progression is unquestionably South Italian, it is probable that the Berlin and former Pozzi statuettes which have been shown to be so closely related to the coin type are South Italian, too.[13]

12. This same statement was made by S. Mirone ("Copies de statues sur les monnaies de la Grande Grèce," *R.N.*, ser. IV, vol. XXVII, 1924, p. 14, pl. 1) as what may be called a theoretical contention, since he offered no tangible evidence in support of his opinion, apparently being unaware of the existence of these statuettes. Mirone thought that the two Metapontine types discussed in this study indicated that toward the mid-fifth century a new school developed in this region under the influence of Polykleitos, and that these statues of Apollo copied on the coins suggest the art of Pythagoras of Rhegion or his circle—a confused and unconvincing idea. For criticism of his position in general, see p. 2, note 10.

13. Of the later works, the earliest, the Kestner statuette, was probably acquired in Italy. So, too, it would seem, was the Bonn statuette, while both the Karlsruhe and Madrid figures come from regions essentially dependent upon Italy.

HERAKLES SEATED

I

THE FIRST of the Italian cities to strike an image of the resting Herakles was Croton. On a series of beautiful staters issued from about 420–390 B.C. (Pl. IX, Fig. 1), the youthful hero relaxes from his labors, sitting at ease upon his lion's skin and looking toward the skyphos held in his outstretched right hand.[1] Usually, his left hand clasps his club, drawing it close to his side as an additional prop for his indolent body.[2] This is Herakles in his legendary rôle as founder of Croton and of the temple of Hera Lakinia.[3] The goddess is shown full face as the obverse type on this issue of staters which apparently celebrates both her worship and that of the hero associated with her cult.

The highly plastic quality of the reverse type, the rendering of the vigorous body, suggests the likelihood that this numismatic image reflects a statuary prototype. Such details as the inclination of the head, the lowering of the extended arm until it almost rests upon the right thigh, and the foreshortened left leg appear to be concessions made by a skilled die-cutter in adapting a three-dimensional plastic type to a flat, circular field. This hypothesis is strongly reinforced by the analogy between the numismatic type and a group of statues commonly considered to be replicas of the Herakles Epitrapezios of Lysippos.[4] The relationship is so striking that one is forced to conclude

that Lysippos either based his work upon an earlier numismatic type whose plastic potentialities he divined or, what is far more probable, that he derived his conception from an older statuary type which is also reflected on the coinage of Croton.

The latter alternative receives further support from a marble torso in the Louvre (Pl. IX, Fig. 2).[5] The fragmentary figure is seated on a lion's skin one paw of which dangles beside the left leg precisely as it does on the coin. The additional presence of the lower part of the club guarantees the identity of the figure as Herakles. The backward angle of the preserved fragment of the left arm together with the section of strut adhering to the left thigh indicates that the position of the arm was similar to that on the coin type, as the fragment of the right foot visible on the base proves that the position of the legs was identical. Not only does the torso lean slightly backward in the manner of the coin but, judging by its style, it reflects a work produced in the third quarter of the fifth century B.C.—the period immediately preceding the appearance of the coin type. The fact that the statue shares these qualities with the coin type makes the restoration to it of a youthful head and an extended right arm highly probable. In this case, it would be fair to assume that statu-

It is interesting to note that this analogy was observed by earlier scholars. Cf. Raoul Rochette, "Conjectures archéologiques sur le groupe antique dont faisait partie le torse du Belvédère," *Mémoires de l'Institut Royal de France. Académie des inscriptions et belles lettres*, XV, 1842, p. 289.

For criticism of Luigi Pernier's remarks about this type ("Statuetta di Ercole da Sinalunga," *Scritti in onore di Bartolomeo Nogara*, Vatican City, 1937, pp. 365 ff.) see below p. 51, note 12.

5. Ht: 38 cm. Lacks head, both arms from slightly below the shoulders, entire right leg down to rear part of foot, left leg from below mid-thigh, upper part of club. F. Ravaisson, "L'Hercule Epitrapézios de Lysippe," *G.A.*, X, 1885, p. 38, pl. VIII, No. 1; H. Heydemann, *Pariser Antiken (12. Hallisches Winckelmannsprogramm)*, Halle, 1887, p. 23, No. 41a; S. Reinach, *Voyage archéologique en Grèce et en Asie Mineur sous la direction de M. Philippe Le Bas*, Paris, 1888, p. 123 and pl. CXLIV; *idem, Répertoire*, II¹, p. 228, No. 2; Paul Weizsäcker, "Zum Herakles Epitrapezios," *Jahrbuch*, IV, 1889, p. 111; M. Collignon, *Lysippe*, Paris, 1904, p. 62; A. Springer and A. Michaelis, *Handbuch der Kunstgeschichte*, Leipzig, I, 1907, pp. 296–297, fig. 543.

1. Grose, No. 1711–14, pl. LIV, 15–18. Rev: ΚΡΟΤΩΝΙΑΤΑΣ around from left; below, strung bow. Obv: Head of Hera nearly facing, inclined to right; hair waving loosely about face; wearing crown ornamented with honeysuckle and ring decoration. A similar date is indicated for the type by George MacDonald, *Catalogue of Greek Coins in the Hunterian Collection*, Glasgow, 1899, I, p. 131, and implied by Head, *H.N.*, pp. 96–97. Pl. IX, Fig. 1A from an example in the collection of the American Numismatic Society; Fig. 1B from Naville Sale Catalogue XV, July 1930, No. 242.

2. However, Grose, No. 1708, club above to left.

3. For the sources on Herakles as founder of this temple cf. G. Giannelli, *Culti e miti della Magna Grecia*, Florence, 1924, pp. 171 ff. For discussion of this temple see Robert Koldewey and Otto Puchstein, *Die griechischen Tempel in Unteritalien und Sicilien*, Berlin, 1899, pp. 41 ff.

4. For bibliography on this type see Waldhauer, *Die antiken Skulpturen der Ermitage*, I, p. 32, No. 14, and below, note 5.

Fig. 2. Paris, Louvre: Marble Statuette of Herakles from Smyrna

Fig. 3. Paris, Louvre: Marble Statuette of Herakles

Fig. 1A. New York, American Numismatic Society: Reverse of Stater of Croton

Fig. 1B. Reverse of Stater of Croton. Present Whereabouts Unknown

Fig. 4. Paris, Ecole des Beaux-Arts: Cast of a Statuette of Herakles

Fig. 5. Leningrad, Hermitage: Marble Statuette of Herakles

PLATE IX

ette and coin alike were reflections of a famous statue honoring the hero-founder.

Ravaisson cited the figure along with a second marble statuette in the Louvre[6] (Pl. IX, Fig. 3) and a cast in the Ecole des Beaux-Arts[7] (Pl. IX, Fig. 4) as among the extant copies of the Herakles Epitrapezios of Lysippos.[8] Such a grouping is unwarranted, for the statuette now under consideration (Pl. IX, Fig. 2) differs from the other two (Pl. IX, Figs. 3, 4) in that its torso is more upright in position, taller and narrower in proportion, deeper in the chest, and more severe in conception. Two stylistically different, if typologically similar, statuary types are visible here as Picard, too, has noted.[9] Waldhauer rightly recognized the second Louvre statuette and the Beaux-Arts cast as related to a marble statuette in the Hermitage[10] (Pl. IX, Fig. 5). To these he added a bronze statuette in Constantinople,[11] considering all four to be replicas of the Herakles Epitrapezios described by Martial[12] and Statius.[13] Both the style and the type of these figures are compatible with such an attribution. Waldhauer considered it reasonable to assume that the one point left uncertain in the ancient descriptions—whether or not the head was bearded—was clarified by the bearded heads of both the Constantinople bronze and the Beaux-Arts cast.[14]

Even if the first Louvre statuette (Pl. IX, Fig. 2) were restored with a bearded head, its fundamental stylistic antecedence to this group would hold good. Yet no indication for such a restoration exists. Hence, the most probable explanation of these interrelationships is that both the Louvre statuette and the coin type (Pl. IX, Figs. 1, 2) reproduce a statue which once stood in Croton and was sufficiently celebrated both in itself[15] and through its reflections to provide the fourth-century sculptor with a basic type upon which to model his own more advanced work. It is difficult to account for the marked similarities between the coin type and this group by other means. In any case, the existence of both fifth- and fourth-century statues of this variety indicates the presence and persistence of a statuary type which, given the statuesque appearance of the coin type, surely served as the basis for the numismatic design.[16]

6. No. 151. Ht: 35 cm. Ravaisson, *op. cit.*, pl. VIII, 2; Heydemann, *op. cit.*, p. 23, No. 41b; Weizsäcker, *loc. cit.*; Collignon, *op. cit.*, p. 62 and fig. 13; Reinach, *Répertoire*, II¹, p. 228, No. 5.

7. Ht: 46 cm. Ravaisson, *op. cit.*, p. 37 and pl. VII; Heydemann, *op. cit.*, p. 23, No. 41c. The cast was presumably of a statue in Rome. ,

8. For additional discussion of this type see notes 4–7 and F. P. Johnson, *Lysippos*, Durham, 1927, pp. 98–104.

9. "L'Heraclès Epitrapezios de Lysippe," *R.A.*, ser. IV, vol. XVII, 1911, p. 268 and note 5. However, he did not attempt to account for these differences, being primarily interested in the second Louvre statuette which he considered a replica of the original Lysippan figure.

10. No. 14. Inv. 19071. Ht: 46 cm. Fine-grained white marble, probably Carrara. Restored: forepart of base with legs, right to above knee, left to below knee; head and most of neck; both arms; tail and paws of skin. Superficially polished with acid (*op. cit.*, No. 14, p. 32, pl. XII).

11. Georg Treu, *Die Bildwerke von Olympia in Stein und Thon* (E. Curtius and F. Adler, *Olympia*, III) Berlin, 1897, p. 236, fig. 263.

12. *Epigrams*, IX, 43; cf. IX, 44.

13. *Silvae*, IV, 6.

14. The more bulbous modelling of the Beaux-Arts cast, its rather baroque quality, suggests that it reproduces a Hellenistic copy, whereas the Hermitage statuette is Antonine. Waldhauer, *loc. cit.*, is certainly right in eliminating the numerous other statues loosely ascribed to this group.

15. In this connection, it is worthy of note that Head, *H.N.*, p. 100, calls the temple of Hera Lakinia the most renowned sanctuary in Italy. Under the circumstances, it is not surprising that the Louvre statuette (Fig. 2) is a Roman copy found in Smyrna.

16. The popularity of this numismatic type is apparent in its almost literal reappearance on the coinage of Herakleia. Cf. Eunice Work, *The Earlier Staters of Heraclea Lucaniae* (*Numismatic Notes and Monographs*, No. 91), New York, 1940, pl. I, figs. 1–2. Head, *H.N.*, p. 71 dates this type 400–370 B.C. Whether one accepts this early fourth-century date or, because of the supposedly initial position of the type within the die sequences of Herakleia, prefers a late fifth-century date contemporaneous with that of the Croton stater does not alter the undoubted dependence of the Herakleia coin on the Croton type. The chief difference between the coins is presented by the club: grasped in the left hand by the Croton Herakles, lying beside the figure on the Herakleia coin. It is understandable that on a variant of the primary, Croton type, the club might be shifted to the field; that it could be an attribute lying in the foreground and later virtually picked up and inserted in the hero's hand is less likely! Furthermore, the association of the plastic works discussed above with the Croton rather than the Herakleia type is assured by the very fact that the statuary varieties invariably grasp the club. Nor is it surprising that the coinage of long-established Croton should influence its newly-founded neighbor. Note, too, the apparently unique Croton coin published by Imhoof-Blumer, *Monnaies grecques*, pl. A, 5 and p. 7, which is itself a variant of the major Croton type and may constitute a connecting link between the Croton and the Herakleia types.

The predilection for representing Herakles drinking in a semireclining attitude must have been marked in this region. See, too, such a different yet related type as the marble torso in Taranto, *Notizie degli scavi*, XXII, 1897, pp. 227–229.

The tetrobol of Salamis current from 411–374/3 B.C. bearing a seated Herakles on its obverse (G. F. Hill, *Catalogue of the Greek Coins of Cyprus* [*A Catalogue of the Greek Coins in the British Museum*, XV], London, 1904, pl. XI, No. 18) is not to be confused with the type of the Croton stater since, in addition to differing in lesser details, it represents another iconographic type where the figure is designed to be seen from the left.

LATE IN the fifth century B.C., Croton struck a stater commemorating its heroic founder Herakles.[1] Nude and beardless, he sits facing left on a rock covered with a lion's skin (Pl. x, Fig. 1). His left hand rests upon his club; his right is outstretched and holds a laurel or olive branch, tied with a knotted fillet, over a flaming altar.[2] Behind him, his bow and quiver[3] and the inscription ΟΙΚΙΣΤΑΣ in archaic letters occupy the right field. The assumption that a statuary type lies behind the coin is inevitable given the appearance of the figure and the historic tradition it reflects.[4] Among the known representations of the seated Herakles, there exists a small group of plastic works typologically related to the Croton stater. Investigation of this group throws considerable light on the genesis of the coin type.

Foremost among them is the colossal Herakles Altemps (Pl. x, Fig. 2).[5] The impression of freshness, of unbroken strength, characteristic of this figure of the youthful hero sets it apart from the normal representations of the mature, fatigued Herakles and, together with a certain majesty, has

suggested the idea that the statue reproduced a cult image.[6] Once the restorations are removed,[7] the statue is seen to be remarkably like the Croton stater in its representation of the youthful beardless hero seated on a rock covered with a lion's skin, his left arm lightly clasping the club, his right outstretched. It differs from the coin in the position of the left leg and in its lack of preservation of the original attribute of the right hand. The enormously awkward prop supporting the right hand as well as the modest strut connecting the club with the left forearm indicate that the Herakles Altemps is a copy of a bronze original. Had this original held a branch comparable to that on the Croton stater, the copyist would have been forced either to add the attribute in bronze or to change it entirely. In either case, no trace of the original attribute remains. Given the precedent of the coin type, it is reasonable to restore to the extended right hand a branch, an attribute well suited to the god-like dignity of the figure.[8]

The Herakles Altemps has long been considered a copy of a late work by Myron or one of his circle.[9] A careful examination of the statue makes such an attribution extremely untenable. Consider, for example, the head (Pl. x, Fig. 3). Compared with such a work as the Palazzo Riccardi

---

1. Diodorus Siculus, IV, 24, 7, tells of the hero's accidental killing of Croton, and of his prophecy that a famous city would arise and bear his name. Ovid, *Metamorphoses*, XV, 7 ff. gives a seemingly different version according to which Herakles, after enjoying Croton's hospitality, prophesied that the city of his descendants would lie on the borders of Lacinium. Theoretically, the two versions are compatible.

2. In exergue: two fishes. Reverse: Tripod, on one side of which Apollo shoots an arrow at Python on the other side. Varieties of the city name. Wt: 121.2 (7.85). Head, *Guide*, p. 25, pl. XIV, No. 18. For bibliography on the question whether the reverse type reproduces a group by Pythagoras of Rhegion mentioned by Pliny, *Historia Naturalis*, XXXIV, 59, see Mirone's discussion in "Copies de statues sur les monnaies de la Grande Grèce," *R.N.*, ser. IV, vol. XXVII, 1924, pp. 4 ff. Inasmuch as there is no monumental evidence available for the solution of this problem, it will not be considered here. Pl. x, Fig. 1 from Hill, *Select Greek Coins*, pl. XLII, 1.

3. Bayet, *Les origines de l'Hercule romain*, p. 37 recalled the Pseudo-Aristotelian tradition (*De mir. ausc.* 107) that the Crotonians took Herakles' bow at Macalla and transported it to their temple of Apollo. The reverse type, with the tripod and Apollo shooting at Python, probably induced Bayet to consider the presence of the bow and knotted fillet on the obverse as allusions to Apollo. Given the ritual nature of this scene and the fact that Herakles is so frequently accompanied by the bow and quiver, such an interpretation is unnecessary.

4. The statement that the representation on the coin has the appearance of a cult image has already been made, *ibid.*, pp. 113 ff.

5. P. Arndt in Br.-Br., Nos. 612–613, where bibliography is quoted.

6. *Ibid.*

7. Restorations: nose; forepart of right hand with apples, upper part of prop to right leg; upper part of lion's head with greater part of club; large piece on rear side of left shoulder; left hand and upper part of club seemingly antique; both arms and legs substantially antique despite repeated breaks. Upper part of head once broken; break passes under left and over right eye. Restorations described as difficult to distinguish because of marble. It is stated that undoubtedly the restoration of the right hand and its attributes is unreliable. *Ibid.*

8. The skyphos held by the Herakles Epitrapezios and the lounging hero on the coinage of Croton and Herakleia is part of a totally different concept of Herakles.

9. A. Kalkmann, *Die Proportionen des Gesichts in der griechischen Kunst (Dreiundfünfzigstes Programm zum Winckelmannsfeste*, Berlin, 1893, pp. 74–76; Furtwängler, *Masterpieces*, p. 202; Curtius, Br.-Br., Nos. 601–604, p. 23; *idem, Die antike Kunst*, p. 250, and others. However, previously, in his article on *Herakles* in Roscher, I², cols. 2182–2183, Furtwängler had referred to the Herakles Altemps as Italic. It is interesting to note that Kalkmann pointed out the similarity of the statue and the Croton coin type. The tentative suggestion of Heydemann, *Pariser Antiken*, p. 25, note 4, that *if* the Herakles Altemps holds a cup it may be related to the Herakles Epitrapezios of Lysippos is without any stylistic support.

FIG. 2. Rome, Palazzo Altemps: Colossal Marble Statue of Herakles

FIG. 3. Detail of Fig. 2

FIG. 4. Rome, Arch of Constantine: Hadrianic Medallion

FIG. 1. London, British Museum: Obverse of Stater of Croton

PLATE X

head,[10] the features will be seen to vary in their seemingly Myronic qualities. The brows, and the large full eyes with deep shadow outlining the lids are, indeed, Myronic. So, too, is the shape of the mouth. But the mouth itself, all right when isolated, is too small when set into the face, where it lacks the generosity of the Myronic mouth and assumes a prettified quality. So, too, the overly small, slender triangle of the face is out of character with the full, rounded cranium, and differs from the long, simply-outlined, rather heavy lower face characteristic of Myron. The crudely rendered ears are too small. The hair, instead of adhering to the skull like the flat surface ornament of a massive, broadly outlined head, is rendered in terms of plastic projection and marked light and shade which break the contour line of the head into ripples. Furthermore, there is an exaggerated archaism about the two front rows of curls that is as un-Myronic as the lack of definition of the curls covering the back part of the head. A comparison of the Altemps head with such Myronic works as the Hermitage and Villa Albani heads and the bearded Herakles in the British Museum[11] indicates that the projection of the entire mass of hair is too great. Finally, in the torso, the area above the navel is not divided into the four-part scheme visible in the Marsyas and the Diskobolos. The arch of the ribs, and the ribs themselves are not so un-Myronic in scheme as they are exaggeratedly over-plastic.

Clearly, the Herakles Altemps is not Myronic. The peculiarities cited in regard to the head—the combination of a small, pointed, triangular lower face with a full cranium, the catching of certain details such as the eyes and mouth which, however, are united in an un-Myronic artificial scheme, together with the archaistic curls—reflect an effort on the part of a later artist to work in the manner of an earlier, more severe style. The forthright vigor and masculinity of the original style have been dissipated. The over-developed plastic delineation of the muscles of the torso is the work of an artist familiar with the naturalistic anatomy of post-Myronic sculpture. Similarly,

the realistic rendering of the lion's face exceeds the conventions of classical art. The only possible explanation of such a style is that a classicizing artist used a severe original of about 450–440 B.C. as the basis for a new work. Both his conception of that period and his actual removal from it are reflected in his treatment of the head, and in his exaggerated attempt to schematize the torso muscles.

Given the marked parallelism between the Croton stater and the colossal statue, and bearing in mind the important fact that, with the possible exception of one bronze statuette, no other existing figure is iconographically comparable either to the representation on the coin or to the statue, it is logical to assume that the severe original which served as the point of departure for the Herakles Altemps was a statue of the hero in Croton, and that that same statue also appears on the city's coinage. On the coin, too, the original statue was subjected to certain predictable modifications. The severe bronze archetype was brought up-to-date, with the result that its representation on the coin looks a generation later. There is ample precedent for such a renovation, as the die sequences of Poseidonia bearing the striding Poseidon indicate. Furthermore, the coin type is the work of a master craftsman who adapted the statue to the coin by means of the most subtle modifications. Thus the head is slightly lowered, the branch is twisted up and back to balance the curving left arm, the contours of the face are fuller, rounder, in an attempt to emphasize the circular shape of the coin and to create the sense of a revolving movement, of a contained composition.[12]

Iconographically, however, the coin type is no doubt faithful to the archetype in all details. Thus the position of the legs—extended evenly before the body—must be that of the original statue. This is the sole iconographic detail in which the Herakles Altemps differs from the coin. The colossal figure is shown with his left leg drawn back—a simple device for enlivening the figure. Such a modification suggests that the marble statue reproduces a Hellenistic version of the prototype.

10. Br.-Br., No. 361.
11. Hermitage No. 65; Villa Albani, No. 744; British Museum, No. 1734. For convenience, cf. illustrations in Furtwängler, *Masterpieces*, figs. 73–75.

12. In connection with the style of this stater, Head, *H.N.*, p. 96 pointed out that Zeuxis was painting at Croton toward the end of the fifth century. It is possible that the presence there of a free pictorial style might have stimulated these modifications.

That the Herakles Altemps is itself that free Hellenistic variant of a fifth-century statue is improbable. The clumsiness of the supports noted before indicates that it is the work of a mediocre sculptor translating a bronze original into a marble copy. That such a sculptor would be capable of making a free copy of an older work is unlikely. Apparently, the Augustan date of the Herakles Altemps[13] is right, and the colossal statue is a routine copy of a late Hellenistic bronze variant of a severe original.[14]

A small bronze statuette in the Louvre[15] reinforces a late Hellenistic date for this bronze variant. A youthful, beardless Herakles is seated on a rock covered with a lion's skin (Fig. 9). His right leg is drawn up in order to support his right arm on which he leans; his left leg is outstretched, while his left arm, now broken at the wrist, was

originally raised to grasp a club. Inasmuch as this appears to be the only other plastic representation of the youthful Herakles seated on a skin-covered rock leaning on his club in this fashion, it would seem that it must be related to the same archetype. Most probably, it is a genre transformation of the sober, monumental statue, retaining the essentials of its position but modifying it into an easy, naturalistic pose. Like the Herakles Altemps and its immediate predecessor, it reflects the same manneristic taste for heightening tension and variety by drawing one leg sharply back and, in this case, turning the head, too, sharply aside. It appears to be late Hellenistic and, in contrast with the archaizing variant reproduced by the Herakles Altemps, this bronze statuette reflects a baroque current in Hellenistic art.[16]

It is altogether possible that the heroic statue of Herakles as founder of Croton indirectly inspired another famous work. One of the Hadrianic reliefs on the Arch of Constantine repro-

13. Br.-Br., Nos. 612–613.
14. Although it is impossible to ascribe the archetype to a known artist, it is tempting, considering both the locale of the work and the stylistic confusion with Myron, to suggest the possibility of a connection with Pythagoras of Rhegion.
15. Ht: 8.7 cm. Blackish-green patina. Provenance not recorded. A. de Ridder, *Bronzes antiques du Louvre*, Paris, I, 1913, No. 651, pl. XLV.

16. For an additional, pictorial reflection of the Herakles Altemps or its original, see W. Klein, "Zum Grundproblem der pompejanischen Wandmalerei," *J.O.A.I.*, XIII, 1910, pp. 139 ff. and figs. 69–70.

FIG. 9. Paris, Louvre: Bronze Statuette of Herakles

duces a figure of the youthful Herakles seated in the midst of his trophies[17] (Pl. x, Fig. 4). It is generally recognized that this relief represents an actual statue. In fact, the existence of several fragmentary marble statuettes,[18] obviously copies of such a statue, and a similar representation of Herakles on Hadrianic coinage[19] prove the point. It is beyond the scope of the present problem to discuss the circumstances attending the erection of this statue or to attempt to find the precise moment in Hadrian's career most suitable for such a commemoration.[20] However, it is worth noting the suggestion that this commemorative statue was a fusion of older types; of an older type of Herakles, best exemplified by the Croton OIKIΣTAΣ, with the hero seated in the midst of his arms.[21] The closest parallel to this statue is the Herakles Altemps.[22] It is hard to believe that the Herakles Altemps would have directly inspired such an adaptation. But it is quite probable that the free Hellenistic copy which the Herakles Altemps reflects served as the point of departure for the later Roman statue represented on Hadrianic coinage and on the Arch of Constantine.[23]

Clearly, then, the Croton stater is based upon a statue of Herakles as the heroic founder of the city.[24] That this archetype was produced about 450–440 B.C. and later served as the basis for a free Hellenistic variant made by a classicizing artist whose work is known only in an Augustan marble copy, the Herakles Altemps, seems equally likely. The powerful impression created by both the original and its Hellenistic variant is implied in their apparent influence on the formation of a third type reflected in the art of the Hadrianic period.

17. Arndt in Br.-Br., No. 565.
18. C. L. Visconti, "Di un frammento marmoreo con relievi appartenente ad una statua di Marte sedente," *Bul. Com.*, xv, 1887, pp. 299 ff., pls. xvii, xviii, said the original of the relief was a famous statue known in copies in the Galeria Lapidaria of the Vatican (No. 25), in the Visconti collection, and from the Via Leonina (Visconti's belief that the original was a colossal Mars by Skopas may be discarded since the statue is clearly a Herakles). E. Petersen, "I rilievi tondi dell'arco di Costantino," *R.M.*, iv, 1889, pp. 336 ff., mistakenly added another statuette in Liverpool and the Herakles Altemps to this list. As Arndt noted, *loc. cit.*, neither of the two actually represents this type of youthful Herakles surrounded by his trophies, nor may they be considered copies of this lost type. J. Sieveking, "Die Medallions am Konstantinsbogen," *R.M.*, xxii, 1907, p. 358, note 2, suggested that the original might have been a portable cult statue belonging to the imperial household.
19. Harold Mattingly and E. A. Sydenham, *The Roman Imperial Coinage*, London, 1926, ii, p. 358, No. 148–150.
20. See the discussions of Arndt. *loc. cit.*, and H. Bulle, "Ein Jagddenkmal des Kaisers Hadrian," *Jahrbuch*, xxxiv, 1919, pp. 149 ff., who identified the statue as Hercules Gaditanus. For discussion of the meaning of this tondo and the entire cycle of medallions see H. P. L'Orange and A. von Gerkan, *Der spätantike Bildschmuck des Konstantinsbogens*, Berlin, 1939, pp. 169 ff.

21. Petersen, *loc. cit.*
22. The remarkable physiognomic similarity between the lion's head of the Herakles Altemps and the curious skin to the right of Herakles on the relief constitutes an additional detail in favor of deriving the two works from a common source.
23. Furtwängler, *Masterpieces*, pp. 202 ff., who considered the original of the Herakles Altemps to be a statue by Myron standing in Rome, also believed that it was the basis of the later type of Herakles seated amid his trophies.
24. A rather similar figure of Herakles appears on a fourth-century red-figured plate from Olynthos (D. M. Robinson, *Excavations at Olynthus*, Part v, Baltimore, 1935, No. 111, pp. 95 ff., pl. lxvii). Despite such differences as the position of the legs, and the presence of a chlamys over the left arm, it gives the impression of reflecting a related fourth-century statuary type which may be a further development of the Croton type.

FIGS. 3–4. Munich, Antiquarium: Bronze Statuette Found in Feurs

FIG. 1. London, British Museum: Reverse of Didrachm of Thermae Himerenses

FIG. 5. Florence, Museo Archeologico: Bronze Statuette of Herakles

FIG. 2. Leningrad, Hermitage: Marble Statuette of Herakles

PLATE XI

III

AFTER THE Carthaginian destruction of Himera in 408 B.C., a remnant of its population established a new settlement at the hot springs on the outskirts of their former home. The new city was known as Thermae Himerenses. Here, according to tradition,[1] the wearied Herakles was refreshed in the course of his Sicilian journey by warm baths which gushed forth at the command of the nymphs. Apparently, the new city deferred to this tradition, for sometime after its settlement in 405 B.C. and before 350 B.C.,[2] it issued didrachms bearing the resting hero as the reverse type (Pl. XI, Fig. 1).

Herakles is represented nude, a slender, beardless young man seated facing left on a rocky pile covered with a lion's skin. He leans lightly on his left arm which extends slightly to the side and behind him and rests upon the head of the lion's skin. In his bent right arm he grasps his club. His left leg is somewhat extended, the left foot being turned aside in a three-quarter view; the right drawn back at a sharp angle and resting on the rocky seat. Behind Herakles, in the right field, two other familiar attributes—the bow and quiver —have been inserted as if to complete his characterization. They are placed parallel to the diagonal line of the left arm, and provoke the immediate impression that they are responsible for the curious angle at which Herakles holds his club, for the diagonal line of the club exactly balances the line of the bow and quiver. As a result, the club is held at a most awkward angle in an unsuccessful attempt to fill the ill-balanced quantity of space to the left of the figure. The arbitrariness of this device is strikingly apparent; the club has been pulled forward from its natural position behind the right leg in order to make it more visible, and to correct the compositional defects described above. Nor does the design give the impression of having been created expressly for the circular die. Rather, it has the distinct appearance of a design taken over from some existing type and unsuccess-

fully altered for a new use. An obvious solution of this problem is that the die-cutter represented a contemporary statue of Herakles, modifying it sufficiently to adapt it to the circular field. This theoretical explanation is bolstered by the existence of a fragmentary marble statuette and two bronze variants which make it possible to reconstruct the lost statuary archetype.

The marble statuette, in the Hermitage, represents Herakles seated on a rock covered with a lion's skin (Pl. XI, Fig. 2). His right leg is drawn sharply back; his left undoubtedly was extended, and his outstretched right arm holds the club. Once the restorations, including the bearded head, are subtracted, a figure iconographically identical with the coin type appears.[3] Traces on the left thigh indicate that either the left hand was in a position similar to that on the coin yet drawn close to the thigh or, in this marble copy of a bronze original, a strut connected the arm with the leg. The analogy noted in the legs and the right arm is apparent also in the divisions of the torso, for on both the statuette and the coin there is a second and rather unusual transverse line parallel to that of the pectorals and above the navel, and in both cases the fold over the groin is strongly emphasized.

Given their iconographic identity, the Hermitage statuette and the Thermae coin type are, in all likelihood, reflections of the same statue.[4] In spite of its poor quality, the Hermitage copy is valuable for its preservation of the correct position of the club. Undoubtedly, in the lost archetype, the club was held at this very natural angle. As previously noted, the fact that it would have been practically invisible on the coin if retained at this angle, and the need for filling the left field gave ample motivation for the die-cutter's modification.

A clearer reflection of the style of the lost arche-

1. Diodorus Siculus, IV, 23, 1.
2. Head, *Guide,* pl. XXVI, p. 46, No. 28. Obverse: ⊖EPMITAN. Head of Hera wearing stephane adorned with sea horses, to right; behind, a dolphin. Wt: 129.3 (8.38). Here Pl. XI, Fig. 1. The same type also occurs on contemporary obols (Grose, No. 2309, pl. LXXV, No. 11).

3. No. 15, Inv. 219. Waldhauer, *Die antiken Skulpturen der Ermitage,* No. 15, pp. 33–34, pl. XII. Ht: 0.53 m. Of fine-grained Carrara marble. Restorations: almost the entire left arm (part of the shoulder ancient); almost the entire left leg (now restored in two parts); the right foot with the lower part of the rock and base; the right hand with a great part of the club; the head and neck; the right breast. Right arm repeatedly broken.
4. Since the statuette is made of Carrara marble, it must be of Roman workmanship.

FIG. 10A. Leipzig, University
Museum: Cast of Loeb Statuette

FIG. 10B. Roanne Museum: Cast of Loeb
Statuette

type is to be found in a bronze variant in the Loeb Collection[5] (Pl. XI, Figs. 3, 4). A nude young man is shown seated to the left, his left leg stretched out at ease, his right drawn sharply back. With his left arm he leaned lightly on some kind of support, while his right hand rests on his right thigh and apparently held a missing attribute.

The restoration of this figure offers numerous problems. The tree stump upon which the young man sits is a modern restoration as the arbitrarily created footrest immediately indicates. What type of seat supported the figure originally? Two casts of the statuette, one in the French museum of Roanne (Fig. 10B), the other in the museum of the University of Leipzig (Fig. 10A) show the figure seated on a knobby tree trunk covered with a lion's skin.[6] The left hand rests on the lion's head and,

in the Leipzig cast, the right arm carries a club. The fact that the Roanne cast is broken at the right wrist suggests that originally it was identical with the Leipzig cast in this respect.

Salomon Reinach[7] never doubted the authenticity of the Roanne cast. Together with the fillet about the young man's head, it led him to identify the figure as a Herakles. If, as Sieveking objected,[8] the silhouette of the base is too restless, too baroque in style to be antique, it is not necessary to assume that the base is modern. It could well be the work of a restorer familiar with fragments of the original who, nonetheless, left unavoidable and unmistakable traces of his own less contained style. Otherwise, one has to assume that the cast itself is a reconstruction. In this case, either it was made by someone familiar with fragments of an original base, or at the suggestion of a learned antiquarian, or it is the result of pure chance.

5. Found in Feurs, the Roman Forum Segusiavorum. Ht: 0.265 m. Right hand lacks top joint of index finger; left, the upper two joints of the little fingers. Modern base of bronzed marble. J. Sieveking, *Bronzen, Terrakotten, Vasen der Sammlung Loeb*, Munich, 1930, pp. 2-4, pls. III, IV.

6. In 1899, Reinach published the Roanne cast ("Quelques statuettes de bronze inédites," *R.A.*, ser. III, vol. XXXV, pp. 59-61, and fig. 1 and still later, *Catalogue illustré du Musée des Antiquités Nationales*, Paris, II, 1921, p. 172, fig. 86). He stated that the whereabouts of the original, which had been found in Feurs and later sold, was unknown. In 1924, Sieveking ("Römische Kleinbronzen," *Münchner Jahrbuch der bildenden Kunst*, n. s. I, 1924, pp. 1 ff.) identified the Loeb bronze as the original of the Roanne cast. Aside from the visual proof of this identification, there is

documentary evidence as well, for among his old papers Sieveking found letters describing the Loeb bronze as belonging to a Frenchman living in Hamburg in 1828. The French owner said that the bronze had been found in Feurs. Dr. A. Rumpf of Leipzig informed Sieveking that since 1850 the University museum had been in possession of a second cast. In the following number of the *Münchner Jahrbuch*, I, 2/3, 1924, pp. 73-74, Sieveking acknowledged this cast and, on the basis of photographs showing it at different angles, he modified several of his original statements.

7. *Loc. cit.*

8. *Op. cit.*, p. 73.

50

None of these alternatives is likely. For if either of the first two were correct, i.e., if the bronze had already lost its base and an experiment was made with the cast, surely it would have been communicated to the restorer of the present bronzed marble base and his creation, which has neither archaeological correctness nor grace to recommend it, would have been avoided. Certainly no one would take the trouble to make two reconstructed casts and leave the original untouched. To suggest that the casts reproduce a modern restoration which was itself lost and replaced seems rather fantastic. Therefore, it is logical to accept the casts as typologically faithful to the original appearance of the statuette. The same logic forces one to accept the club preserved in the Leipzig cast as the original attribute of the right hand and arm. By virtue of the club and lion's skin, and of the equally important fillet and swollen ears, the figure is clearly a Herakles.[9]

A comparison of the Loeb bronze (Pl. XI, Fig. 4) corrected by the Leipzig cast (Fig. 10A) with the Thermae coin reveals an exact typological correspondence between the two save for the position of the right arm. Even so far as the placing of the left hand on the head of the lion's skin, the trailing down of the tail beneath Herakles' left leg, the three-quarter angle of his left foot, and the presence of the horizontal fold over the navel are concerned, the correspondence is exact. The most plausible explanation of so marked a similarity is the assumption that the Loeb bronze is a Roman variant of the monumental statue reflected on the coinage of Thermae.[10]

The second variant of the Thermae type is a small bronze statuette in Florence[11] (Pl. XI, Fig. 5). The youthful, beardless hero is seated on a rock and leans sharply backward, glancing up much as he does on the coin. He not only grasps a club in his outstretched right hand, but his legs are quite parallel to the coin type. However, instead of sitting on the lion's skin, he carries it thrown over his left arm, while in his left hand he holds the familiar apples. The fact that of the innumerable representations of the seated hero, the Florentine bronze is the only other piece presenting such similarities to the Thermae type constitutes a reason for considering it a variant of the archetype.[12] Indeed, one of the strongest arguments in

9. The only other attribute that would fit the position of the fingers is the purse commonly held by Hermes. The marked formal similarity between the Loeb bronze and the familiar scheme of the resting Hermes who holds a purse in his hand induced Sieveking to consider the bronze a hybrid type compiled by a Roman Imperial artist. The presence of the fillet and the figure's swollen ears forced him to recognize the statuette as a Herakles even when he discarded the lion's skin base as modern. Thus he believed that by the simple device of modifying the position and attribute of the right hand, a resting Herakles was transformed into a Hermes. It is highly improbable that a compiling Roman artist would have been either so ill-informed or so careless as to retain swollen ears for his Mercury, let alone Sieveking's original suggestion that he retained the lion's skin seat as well. The fact that both the resting Herakles and the seated Hermes were contemporary types is sufficient to explain a natural typological and stylistic similarity. The Loeb bronze was also referred to as a Mercury by Felix Stähelin, *Die Schweiz in römischer Zeit*, Basel, 1931, fig. 104, in a brief comment on a Hellenistic statuette of a seated Mercury found in Augst which is described as based on the prototype of a fourth-century resting Herakles.

10. Sieveking considered the Loeb bronze Julio-Claudian. His opinion that it reflected a monumental Herakles type of the mid-fourth century was certainly right. It is interesting to note that in an attempt to reconstruct this original Herakles type, Sieveking suggested that the outstretched right hand of the hero should lean on a club in the way in which he leans on his bow and quiver on the coinage of Lamia in Thessaly from 302–286 B.C. (Percy Gardner, *Catalogue of the Greek Coins in the British Museum, Thessaly to Aetolia*, I, London, 1883, pl. IV, Nos. 1, 2). Apparently, he did not consider the similar and still more apt didrachm of Thermae—the earliest numismatic example of this Herakles type.

The discrepancy between Sieveking's statement that the bronze reflects a pre-Lysippan style comparable to the Ares Ludovisi or the Herakles Lansdowne, and Reinach's classification of the bronze as Lysippic is dissipated by the hypothesis that the archetype was a local product and, as such, would not fit precisely into the style of any known Greek sculptor. The provenance of the statuette is of no assistance. The fact that it was found in a provincial Roman city probably means that it was brought there by someone who had bought it in Italy. Whether it was actually made in Sicily is of little importance. In any case, the sculptor who made it, whether he worked in Sicily, in Rome, or in the provinces must have been familiar with the lost Thermae statue or one of its copies.

11. Inventory of the Museo Archeologico No. 2439. Published in the *Reale galleria di Firenze*, Florence, 1824, ser. IV, vol. III, pp. 19 ff., pl. CVI, and illustrated and quoted by Luigi Pernier, "Statuetta di Ercole da Sinalunga," *Scritti in onore di Bartolomeo Nogara*, Vatican City, 1937, pp. 365 ff., pl. XLIX. Virtually the same article by Pernier was published under the title "Copie italiche dell'Herakles Epitrapezios di Lisippo" in *Archaiologike Ephemeris*, 1937, pp. 5 ff.

12. Pernier, "Statuetta di Ercole da Sinalunga," *loc. cit.*, who related the Florentine bronze to the general motive of the Herakles Epitrapezios, a motive he described as pre-Lysippan, deriving from the circle of Euphronios and Meidias and translated into sculpture by the school of Pheidias before passing into coinage on the staters of Croton, is exceedingly careless in his lack of differentiation of individual statuary types. To relate such types as these and the bronze Herakles from Pompeii in the Naples Museum in a general typological development is legitimate; but

favor of drawing the Hermitage, Loeb, and Florentine statuettes into so close a relationship to the Thermae didrachm is the very fact that they are unique among statuesque representations of Herakles.[13]

one should not ignore the fact that individually each is a distinct statuary type. Reinach, too, *loc. cit.*, was at fault in this respect, since he considered the Roanne cast, the Florentine bronze, and the Herakles Altemps alike in motif—apparently referring to the fact that all three rest on a club. As the discussion on pp. 43 ff. indicates, the Herakles Altemps belongs to an entirely different type.

13. Whether the lost Thermae archetype was, in turn, dependent upon an earlier Greek statue of Herakles or may be regarded as the first translation into sculpture in the round of a type already well established in painting and relief cannot be ascertained. The existence of the seated Herakles on the Meidias hydria in the British Museum (Furtwängler-Reichhold, *Griechische Vasenmalerei*, Munich, I, 1904, pp. 38 ff., pls. VIII, IX) and a somewhat analogous representation of the hero on a bronze relief plaque from a fourth or third-century tomb in Praeneste (A. della Seta, *Museo di Villa Giulia*, Rome, 1918, I, p. 451, Barberini Collection,

In all probability, Thermae Himerenses commemorated the traditional pause in Herakles' journey with a monumental statue of the resting hero. This lost statue, made relatively early in the fourth century, was apparently reproduced on the city's coinage sometime before 350 B.C. It also survives in a small marble copy in the Hermitage and in two bronze variants which it appears to have inspired.

No. 13221, and pl. LIX; cf. Pierre Wuilleumier, *Tarente*, Paris, 1939, p. 324 for additional bibliography and discussion) suggests the greater probability of the latter alternative.

The marked similarity between the Thermae coin type and a fourth to third-century diobol of Tarentum (*Sylloge Nummorum Graecorum*, II, *The Lloyd Collection*, London, 1933, Pts. I–II, No. 243, pl. VIII) suggests that the latter was inspired by the former. Note, too, a possible reflection of the persistence of this statuary and numismatic type in the coinage of Bactria on the reverse of a coin of Euthydemos, *ca.* 220 B.C. (Head, *Guide*, p. 60, pl. XXXIII, No. 16).

A STANDING HERAKLES AT HERAKLEIA

SHORTLY AFTER the middle of the fourth century B.C., Herakleia in Lucania issued staters bearing as their reverse type a nude figure of Herakles armed with club, bow and arrow, quiver, and lion's skin[1] (Pl. XII, Fig. 1). The hero is represented as a beardless young man. He stands with his weight on his right leg, looks toward his left and, clasping a tall, knobby club in his right hand, he grasps a bow and arrow in his left. A luxuriant lion's skin hangs over his left arm, and he wears a quiver which is visible below his left biceps and further indicated by a baldric running diagonally across his chest from his right shoulder. Late in the fifth century, representations of Herakles began to show him nude, no longer draped in the lion's skin, but carrying it either hanging from or wrapped around his left arm.[2] It is this stage in the development of Herakles-iconography that the Herakleia coin type reflects. The immediate impression created by this type is that it reproduces a statue, an impression justified by the existence of a number of statues and statuettes related to the coin type by close iconographic and stylistic parallels.

Among the sculptures in the Ny Carlsberg Glyptotek is a bronze statue formerly in the Jacobsen collection and reputedly of Roman provenance[3]

(Pl. XII, Figs. 2, 3). Because of the gesture of the left hand, it was once interpreted as a charioteer. However, in view of the leisurely attitude of the figure, such an interpretation is impossible and, as Arndt recognized,[4] the statue is undoubtedly a representation of Herakles, since the position of the left fingers indicates that they were designed to hold a bow and arrow—an explanation corroborated by the clearly visible traces of a baldric stretching over the right shoulder toward the left hip.[5] The lowered right arm and hand obviously held something, too. Arndt preferred a lion's skin to a club for this attribute, probably because he was impressed with the statue's stylistic similarities to the Lansdowne Herakles.[6] His preference is unsatisfactory since the two statues are not only typologically unrelated but, in addition, the

1. ϜΗΡΑΚΛΕΙΩΝ around to right, inwards. Obv: Head of Athena to right in crested Corinthian helmet, on which Scylla hurls stone, with single drop earrings and necklace. For a brief outline of the history of Herakleia, and a study of the die sequences of its coinage see Eunice Work, *The Earlier Staters of Heraclea Lucaniae* (*Numismatic Notes and Monographs*, No. 91), New York, 1940. The coin is included in the period 345–281 B.C. by Grose, I, p. 113; in the period 359–323 B.C. by Regling, *Die antike Münze als Kunstwerk*, pl. XL, No. 827; and appears as the first item in a group dated 335–280 B.C. by Gardner, *The Types of Greek Coins*, p. 181 and pl. XI, No. 1.

2. For the iconography of Herakles see Furtwängler in Roscher, I², cols. 2135 ff. and F. Dürrbach's article "Hercules" in Daremberg and Saglio, *Dictionnaire des antiquités grecques et romaines*, Paris, 1900, III¹, pp. 118 ff.

3. No. 261. Ht: 1.28 m. Bought in Rome in 1891 and said to have been found in the ruins of an ancient foundry under the Via Barberini. Originally published by Paul Arndt, *La Glyptothèque Ny-Carlsberg*, Munich, 1912, pp. 136–137, pls. LXXXIX–XCII; most recent discussion: Frederik Poulsen, *Ny-Carlsberg Glyptotek, Katalog over Antike Skulpturer*, Copenhagen, 1940, p. 193. Also discussed by Furtwängler, *Masterpieces*, p. 299 and note 3; Margarete

Bieber, "Der Paris des Euphranor und Jünglingsköpfe aus dem IV. Jahrhundert v. Chr.," *Jahrbuch*, XXV, 1910, p. 168; T. L. Shear, "Head of Helios from Rhodes," *A.J.A.*, XX, 1916, pp. 294–296; G. Krahmer, "Eine Jünglingsfigur mittelhellenistischer Zeit," *R.M.*, XLVI, 1931, p. 140, note 1; H. K. Süsserott, *Griechische Plastik des 4. Jahrhunderts vor Christus*, pp. 170 ff.; also listed under Br.-Br., No. 691–692, p. 5, No. 39 and illustrated in *Tillaeg til Ny-Carlsberg Glyptotek. Billedtavler af antike Kunstvaerker*, pl. XVIII, No. 261. G. Lippold, *Antike Skulpturen der Glyptothek Ny-Carlsberg*, which apparently discussed this statue on p. 20, is not available to me.

When the statue was discovered, the little finger of the right hand was largely missing, as well as the big toe of the right foot, the second, third, and fourth toes, and greater part of the sole of the left foot. Spots on right forearm and below right knee mended. Numerous faults in casting, especially on rear of left calf, mended in antiquity. Left eye modern; right, blue stone iris set in white material. Lightly engraved circle around nipples. Head, arms, possibly lower part of legs apparently cast separately. Left hand found intact but detached from body. Base of two complete plinths, one superimposed on the other: square step decorated with spirals and eight-rayed stars in each corner, surmounted by a base composed of a scotia between two tori. Base considered to belong to statue although the latter was found separated from it.

4. *Op. cit.*, p. 136.

5. And universally accepted save by Shear and Bieber, *loc. cit.* Shear interpreted the statue as Helios with reins in his left hand and a whip in his right, and associated it with a Rhodian head in his possession. Despite a certain similarity of hair and brow, the slanting, smiling eyes, the parted lips and totally different proportions of the profile make it impossible to relate this winsome head with the sober, forthright Copenhagen bronze. I do not find Margarete Bieber's attempt to relate the statue to the Antikythera bronze convincing.

6. Br.-Br., No. 691–692. Poulsen, *loc. cit.*, repeats this suggestion.

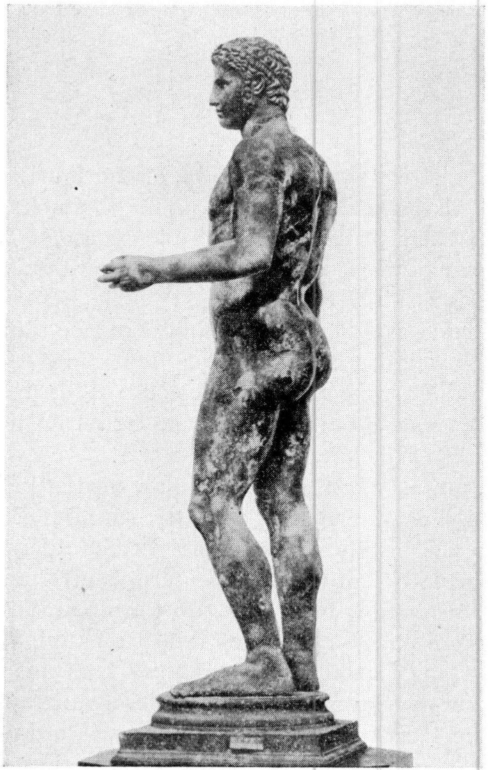

FIGS. 2–3. Copenhagen, Ny Carlsberg Glyptotek: Bronze Statue Found in Rome

FIG. 1. New York, American Numismatic Society: Reverse of Stater of Herakleia

FIG. 4. Syracuse, Regio Museo Archeologico: Marble Statuette of Herakles Found near Syracuse

PLATE XII

effect of a skin dangling limply in the right hand as a balance to a bow and arrow in the left would be extremely unskillful and distasteful. The obvious attribute to restore is the club, thereby aligning the figure with a defined statuary type.[7] Furthermore, one of the most striking iconographic details shared by the Ny Carlsberg figure and the stater type is that quite rare piece of equipment, the baldric. Indeed, the resemblance between the figures is so marked as to assure the correctness of restoring a lion's skin to the left arm, where it would probably have been connected by means of solder which, in the meantime, has disappeared.[8]

The resulting statue of Herakles exactly parallels the Herakleia coin type not only in regard to its attributes but also, and still more conclusively, in general pose, stance, and direction of the head; in the same subtle suggestion of greater weight on the right leg with an equally slight lowering of the left hip; in its emphasis on the pectoral muscles and fold over the groin, and in the strikingly similar contours of the shapely legs. In both cases, the balance between a rather stocky and a lithe figure is marked.

One easily accountable difference separates the figures—the angle of the arms. A die-engraver attempting to recreate the effect of a three-dimensional statue on a flat, circular space must, of necessity, consider the formal restrictions of that space and design accordingly. As Percy Gardner has well said, "in copying a statue on a coin, the position of arms and legs is often modified, in order to make the motive clearer."[9] Hence the forty-five degree projection of the left arm—in itself difficult to render in relief—has been modified in the interest of both design and intelligibility. Similarly, the right arm has been slightly modified and the resulting open line of the arms produces a most harmonious composition given the

shape of the coin. Nevertheless, neither of these changes in any way affects the basic concept.[10]

Whether this youthful Herakles is a fourth-century original of provincial workmanship or a Roman copy of such an original cannot be determined without first-hand investigation of the statue.[11]

Closely related to this bronze statue is a marble statuette in Syracuse[12] (Pl. XII, Fig. 4). It was found in 1909 in a cave north of the suburb Sta. Lucia together with some mediocre Hellenistic sculptures. Orsi conjectured the cave to have been the shop of a modest sculptor, possibly creator of the later works but, in any case, restorer of the fine Herakles. For the statuette was broken in antiquity, and its original marble base was trimmed to an oval and inserted into a second rectangular base of grey marble. The left arm, now broken in the middle of the biceps, was held behind the plane of the chest. Below it, beside the left foot, appears a fragment bearing traces of red—clearly the lower part of the lion's skin. The right arm has a downward-curving open hand. Orsi suggested that this youthful Herakles held apples in his right hand and a club in his left. Obviously, there is no physical necessity for choosing one at-

7. The club could certainly not have rested on the present base which is not only too small for the figure but strangely unlike it in its far greater refinement of workmanship. Given these circumstances and the fact that statue and base were discovered separated from each other in a foundry, it seems altogether possible that the base may not belong. In any case, in a bronze statue the club need not rest on the base, as Arndt and Poulsen, op. cit., implied in their very consideration of the restoration of a club.
8. The fact that the left hand was found detached from the arm makes the loss of such a skin still more understandable.
9. Gardner, "Copies of Statues on Coins," p. 112.

10. The destroyed condition of the face on the coins of this type known to me makes it impossible to use it for comparative purposes. In any case, the better preserved face on the coin illustrated by Regling, loc. cit., strengthens rather than weakens the analogies pointed out between coin and statue.
11. Arndt, loc. cit., thought the statue a copy of an original by Skopas' school or, possibly, after one of the master's works, since he considered that it showed a certain lack of finesse in the execution of the hair, in the rather hard pubic curls, the overly large feet, and the way in which the upper bones of the hand are recurved. Furthermore, he quoted Bulle as saying that the type of base on which the figure stands—a type composed of two complete plinths, one superimposed on the other—is a duplication of elements that does not occur until rather late in the Roman period, no example being known as yet from the first century B.C. However, as we have seen in note 7, the circumstances of the discovery as well as the discrepancy in size and style between statue and base make it very likely that the two were not contemporaneous. Hence, the only means of dating the figure, its own style and workmanship, cannot be verified at the present time.
12. No. 30575. Greek marble. Ht: ca. 50 cm. Preliminary report by P. Orsi, N.S., XXXVII, 1912, pp. 296–298, fig. 7. Chief publication by Orsi, "Statue inedite o malnote di Siracusa," Antike Plastik, Berlin and Leipzig, 1928, pp. 172–175, pl. XII, figs. 4–6. Briefly discussed and illustrated by B. Pace, Arti ed artisti della Sicilia antica, p. 549, note 1, and fig. 57; A. della Seta, Italia antica, p. 158 and fig. 159; G. Libertini, Il Regio museo archeologico di Siracusa, Rome, 1929, p. 164, pl. II. Reproduced by Reinach, Répertoire, V, p. 81, No. 9. Mentioned by Süsserott, op. cit., pp. 192 ff. Pl. XII, fig. 4 from Alinari photo. No. 33381.

FIG. 11. Copenhagen, Ny Carlsberg Glyptotek: Details of Bronze Statue Found in Rome

FIG. 12. Syracuse, Regio Museo Archeologico: Details of Marble Statuette of Herakles Found near Syracuse

tribute rather than another for the left hand, while the right hand is far better shaped to rest on a rounded club than to hold apples, especially since when Herakles does hold apples, his hand is upturned.[13] Furthermore, as we shall see, the statuette is probably pre-Hellenistic, and the type of Herakles holding the apples of the Hesperides did not appear until the Hellenistic age.[14]

Again, the modelling, type, and stance of the figure, its slight obliqueness in response to the curving weight of the body are amazingly close to the coin type. The figure is remarkable for its combination of lithe grace and athletic vigor. Orsi considered it to have been inspired by the Agias group of 338–334 B.C., and to have come from the house of some noble Syracusan of the Hellenistic or Roman period.[15] However, a date in the third quarter of the fourth century, in the very age of Lysippos, seems more in keeping with the stylistic and iconographic characteristics of the statuette and, in addition, not only draws it close to the original period of the coin type, but is a further indication of the incorrectness of Orsi's proposed restoration.[16]

A comparison of the Ny Carlsberg and Syracuse figures immediately reveals not simply a general typological similarity but an extraordinary iden-

tity of silhouette no matter how minute the comparison of curves and of the muscles may be. Note, too (Figs. 11, 12), the short tousled hair, the locks over the forehead, the shape of the forehead and chin, the similar placing of ears, mouth, and the long nose. The figures even share the peculiarity of large feet. The slightly greater relaxation of the Syracuse statuette, the more Lysippic rendering of the torso, together with its less alert, more reflective expression probably result from variations in the copyist's interpretation. Possibly the more energetic appearance of the Ny Carlsberg statue is closer to the coin; possibly a certain Praxitelean tendency crept into the marble copy producing a less individual expression and atmosphere.

The solution of the problem is clear. Both the Ny Carlsberg and Syracuse Herakles must be dependent upon a third statue made about the middle of the fourth century, unless we have the good fortune to possess in the Copenhagen Herakles the very model of the coin. In any case, the archetype was very likely of bronze, since that medium would have been more appropriate for the attributes, as is verified by the fact that the Ny Carlsberg statue, as well as two bronze statuettes which will be discussed shortly—the only copies retaining traces of the bow, baldric, or quiver—are of bronze. A synthesis of the attributes of the two figures enables us to reconstruct the attributes of the archetype, adding to the bow, arrow, quiver, and baldric of the Ny Carlsberg statue, the lion's skin and club of the Syracuse statuette.[17] Indeed, hav-

13. Cf. Herakles Mastai in the Sala Rotonda of the Museo Vaticano, Georg Lippold, *Die Skulpturen des Vaticanischen Museums*, Berlin and Leipzig, III[1], 1936, No. 544, pls. XXXVII, XLIV.
14. Furtwängler in Roscher, I[2], col. 2172.
15. An opinion followed by Pace and Della Seta, *loc. cit.*, and, on the whole, by Libertini, *loc. cit.*, although he considered the ponderation of the figure Polykleitan.
16. See note 14.

17. The bow and arrow, if actually present on the Syracuse statuette, were, of course, added in bronze.

56

ing established the stylistic and typological similarities between the two figures, it is now possible to restore the lion's skin and club to the Ny Carlsberg statue with even greater certainty.

The resulting archetype appears in every respect identical with the Herakleia coin type. Clearly, the type itself reflects a famous contemporary statue of sufficient importance not only to have served as the city's emblem but also to have been repeatedly copied, as will be seen. Whether this statue was a cult image or served some other purpose it is impossible to say. However, the reason why the Ny Carlsberg Herakles has been variously considered a copy of a statue by Skopas,[18] a work by a fourth-century artist whose essentially Polykleitan style nevertheless reflects the contemporary influence of Lysippos,[19] or, again, a classicistic figure made on the basis of fourth-century style[20] is apparent: undoubtedly, the archetype was a provincial work, the creation of a local South Italian or Sicilian artist affected by the style of his great contemporaries. Hence, the Ny Carlsberg statue, as well as the Syracuse statuette, may be considered works of this region.[21]

The widespread popularity of the archetype is attested by the existence of a considerable number of additional statues and statuettes both contemporary and later, with and without modifications.

A statuette in Syracuse offers the next close parallel to the Herakleia coin type.[22] A glance at a sketch of this figure (Pl. XIII, Fig. 5) reveals such close stylistic and iconographic similarities to both the preceding Syracuse statuette and the coin type (Pl. XII, Figs. 1, 4) that it may be safely assigned to the group. The identification as Herakles is guaranteed by the lion's skin.[23]

A statuette of Pentelic marble found in the Roman Campagna[24] bearing a lion's skin over the left arm and having the remains of a club on the base to the right of the figure also appears to reflect the Herakleia type of Herakles (Pl. XIV, Fig. 6). The figure is strikingly close to the Ny Carlsberg statue, as a comparison of the silhouette, the modelling of the torso and legs, and the conspicuously large feet indicate (cf. Pl. XII, Figs. 2, 3 and Pl. XIV, Fig. 6). The loss of freedom in the position of the left arm is to be expected in a marble copy. On the other hand, the position of the raised left foot, placed slightly to the rear, is more closely related to the Syracuse than to the Ny Carlsberg figure. The long legs contrast with the thick-set, severely emphasized torso and, together with its general effect of relaxed ease, suggest an eclectic work combining a certain fifth-century stockiness with a fourth-century litheness. These very characteristics strengthen the relationship between the statuette and the group.

Two other small bronze statuettes, both of inferior quality, nonetheless reflect the same icono-

18. Arndt, op. cit., p. 136; cf. Furtwängler, Masterpieces, p. 299 and Curtius, Die antike Kunst, p. 382.

19. Süsserott, op. cit., p. 170.

20. Krahmer and Poulsen, loc. cit.

21. G. Cultrera, "Una statua di Ercole," Memorie delle R. Accademia dei Lincei, Classe di scienze morali, storiche e filologiche, Rome, ser. v, vol. XIV, fasc. III, 1910, pp. 180 ff., related the Herakles Albertini to the Ny Carlsberg statue, considering them dependent upon the same type. (See, too, Bieber and Poulsen, loc. cit., who also considered the works related.) Seen from the front, the Herakles Albertini may seem to fit this scheme. However, when seen from its right side, as in Cultrera's pl. II, it is clear that it does not belong to the Ny Carlsberg type. For below the hip, on the right thigh about in line with the right buttock, is a somewhat oval break on the surface of the leg. Since the right arm is broken below the shoulder, and the only trace of the club is the knobby base, it is apparent that the statue held the club in its right hand, and that the right hand leaned against the thigh as it does in the Ludovisi Herakles illustrated here on Pl. I, fig. 6. Here the club makes an angle against the body and rests on a low stony support, rather than standing directly on the ground as it does in the Ny Carlsberg Herakles type. Hence this statuette is automatically eliminated from the present discussion. Similarly, without seeing a side view of Cultrera's fig. 2, it is impossible to state whether the Herakles from the villa of Voconius Pollio in the Museo Nazionale in Rome should or should not be included in the Herakleia group. See Helbig-Amelung, Führer durch die öffentlichen Sammlungen klassischer Altertümer in Rom, II, 2, No. 1246.

22. In 1939, in Room VII of the Regio Museo Archeologico. Seemingly unnumbered. Greek marble. Preserved ht: 52 cm. Badly destroyed, lacking head, right arm from biceps down, left hand, right leg below knee, left leg from the middle of the calf, and the lower part of the lion's skin. Traces of a strut are visible on the exterior of the right thigh, indicating the necessity of bracing the right wrist.

Because of the conditions prevailing in Syracuse late in August, 1939, I was unable to obtain any information about this figure from the Museum authorities.

23. It is possible that a bronze statuette ca. 12 cm. high in the case known as the Antiquarium on the second floor of this museum may also belong to the group. The general disposition of the figure, the fact that both hands obviously held something, together with the apparently fourth-century style of this inferior piece are compatible with such an attribution.

24. G. Annibali, N.S., LX, 1935, p. 79, fig. 3. Preserved height: 76 cm. Lacks head, right forearm and attribute; right leg restored from knee to top of foot.

graphic type. A figure in the Museo Biscari[25] in Catania (Pl. XIII, Fig. 7), repeats the type even to such details as the left foot posed slightly behind the right, the set of the head, and the curving line of the outstretched right hand as it grasps the upper part of a club of which only the top remains. The left arm, over which the now fragmentary skin hangs, is broken in the mid-forearm but indicates by its poise and direction that it held something. Although the quality of the work is too poor to merit a minute stylistic analysis, it does retain a certain springy vitality of pose suggestive of intense potential energy. Apparently, it is a Hellenistic replica of the famous statue. No provenance is given for the statuette. However, its connection with the previously discussed works suggests that it is a product of the region, an attribution borne out, in this instance, by the high probability that such a mediocre minor work is of local origin.

The second bronze statuette, in Paris[26] (Pl. XIII, Fig. 8), is again interesting as a reflection of the Herakleia type in which both the chief iconographic characteristics and a certain slender litheness are retained. It is also useful in documenting the existence of the bow since, although it has now disappeared, it surely was once present. Again, it would be profitless to discuss the details of this poor Roman work. As in the preceding case, it is doubtless a South Italian piece.[27]

The importance and popularity of the archetype of the Herakleia coin are further indicated by several Roman statues which, despite modifications, are probably dependent upon it.

The first, in the Palazzo Pitti in Florence, is an over life-size marble statue of unknown provenance[28] (Pl. XIII, Fig. 9). Once its restorations are removed, the figure presents an exact iconographic parallel to the coin type. A sixteenth-century drawing[29] of the statue before it had suffered its present restorations preserves a still closer aspect (Pl. XIII, Fig. 10) in which the curve of the right arm and the curious position of the left hand are clearly dependent upon the Herakleia archetype. Indeed, the rendering of the left hand is so much more suggestive of the technique of the draughtsman than of the sculptor, that it is tempting to suppose that when the drawing was made the hand had already been broken from the statue, leading the draughtsman to the present improvisation. In any case, the restorer who supplied a hand to the incomplete left arm replaced the missing member by the familiar hand clasping three apples. Otherwise, it is necessary to assume that the lost hand, too, was an invention of a copyist forced to eliminate from his marble replica the bow of the bronze original. The drawing also suggests the original proper position of the head which at present appears ill-suited to the body.[30]

A comparison of this statue with the Ny Carlsberg and Syracuse figures (Pl. XII, Figs. 2–4, and text Figs. 11–12) indicates that the silhouette of the figure and its general anatomical rendering are close to theirs despite the presence of certain more advanced details such as the treatment of the ribs. The close-cropped, impressionistically rendered hair with its short locks framing a narrow rectangular forehead, the sunken temples, the straggling sideburns, the slightly swelled ears, and the profile are striking in their repetition of details characteristic especially of the Ny Carlsberg head. These similarities, reinforcing the basic typological identity of the statue and the coin type, make it highly probable that the Pitti figure is a Roman copy of the Herakleia archetype. The few more

25. G. Libertini, *Il Museo Biscari*, Milan and Rome, 1930, p. 91, pl. XLIV, 229. Inv. No. 594; ht: 10.4 cm.

26. Babelon and Blanchet, *Catalogue des bronzes antiques de la Bibliothèque nationale*, p. 229, No. 547. Ht: 16.3 cm.

27. Two small bronze statuettes in the British Museum (Walters, *Catalogue of the Bronzes*, p. 217, Nos. 1278, 1280) exactly correspond to the Herakleia type, according to Walters' description. Unfortunately, they are not illustrated. However, No. 1280 is especially interesting as possessing all of the required attributes. The provenance of both statuettes is unknown. On theoretical grounds, they may be associated with the Herakleia type and attributed to the same region.

28. Ht: 1.95 m. Of Greek marble. Restorations: Nose, little piece of neck, right forearm, greater part of club, left hand with apples, surrounding part of lion's skin, left knee. Upper lip and edges of ears broken. Supposedly brought to the Palazzo Pitti from the Villa Medici in Rome. Arndt, *Einzelaufnahmen*, Nos. 228–230; H. Dütschke, *Antike Bildwerke in Oberitalien*, Leipzig, 1875, II, No. 33.

29. S. Reinach, *L'album de Pierre Jacques*, Paris, 1902, pl. 74 bis, drawn in Rome in the last third of the sixteenth century. Reinach, p. 133, suggested the identity of the drawing and the Pitti Herakles.

30. Arndt, *Einzelaufnahmen*, loc. cit., felt unable to vouch that the head belonged to the body. There is no indication to the contrary. The solution of his uncertainty is supplied both by the drawing and by the breaks at the neck which show that the head has been restored to the body at an incorrect angle.

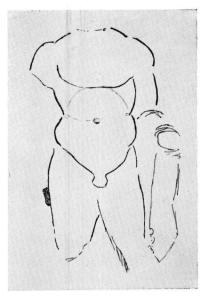

FIG. 5. Syracuse, Regio Museo Archeologico: Marble Statuette of Herakles

FIG. 13. Carnuntum: Marble Statue of Herakles from Carnuntum

FIG. 8. Paris, Bibliothèque Nationale: Bronze Statuette of Herakles

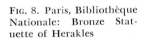

FIG. 7. Catania, Museo Biscari: Bronze Statuette of Herakles

FIG. 9. Florence, Palazzo Pitti: Marble Statue of Herakles

FIG. 10. Drawing of the Palazzo Pitti Herakles by Pierre Jacques

PLATE XIII

FIG. 6. Marble Statuette of Herakles from the Campagna di Roma

FIG. 11. Rome, Palazzo Colonna: Marble Statue of Herakles

FIG. 12. Rome, Museo di Villa Borghese: Marble Statue

PLATE XIV

advanced details of the torso are unconscious modifications of the copyist, as the cumbersome support was a conscious device necessitated by the translation from bronze into marble.[31]

Another replica of the type is to be found in an over life-size statue of unknown date and provenance in the Palazzo Colonna in Rome[32] (Pl. XIV, Fig. 11). Once the head and other restorations are removed, such parts as are left fit the Herakleia type and, if the bad condition of the figure allows one to judge, its style suggests an original of that period. Again the ill-arranged support connecting skin and thigh bespeaks a bronze original. Hence this statue may well have been a Roman copy of the Herakleia type which, becoming damaged, was later repaired. The restorer repaired the figure as Herakles with the apples of the Hesperides. Such a modification might even have taken place in the Roman period since the extreme popularity of the Herakles-with-the-apples type in the Hellenistic and Roman periods was sufficient to cause a confusion or mingling of the types, especially at the hands of the Roman copyist who, according to Furtwängler,[33] had a predilection for that motive.[34]

A more removed quotation of the Herakleia type may be seen in the Herakles of the Villa Borghese Casino[35] (Pl. XIV, Fig. 12). Again, the subtraction of restorations removes all contradictory elements save the head which seemingly belongs, and is a third century A.D. Roman portrait. Hence the statue is apparently a Roman portrait figure honoring a man by representing him as Herakles, and basing the representation of Hera-

kles upon the Herakleia type which we thus see faintly reflected by a late admirer. Here, too, the awkward treatment of the skin suggests a bronze original.

A related case is the marble figure from Carnuntum[36] (Pl. XIII, Fig. 13) showing Herakles with traces of a crown or fillet falling on his shoulders, with the usual club and lion's skin and, below the club, a bull's head. The statue is of careful post-Hadrianic workmanship, according to Studniczka, who accepted Hirschfeld's conjecture that it is a representation of the Emperor Commodus who, Lampridius states, was called a Roman Hercules and allowed himself to be represented as such in statues.[37] Although in the poor drawing the style and anatomy of the figure seem more advanced—easily the result of the copyist—in pose and attitude it reflects the Herakleia type. Like the Villa Borghese statue, it may ultimately derive from the same archetype, in which case its later transformations and additions would afford striking proof of the importance of the original statue.[38]

31. Arndt's opinion, *ibid.*, that the original work was probably Skopaic, falls into the same category as that voiced in regard to the Ny Carlsberg statuette, *op. cit.*, pp. 84–85.

32. Amelung in *Einzelaufnahmen*, No. 1136. Ht: 2.03 m. Of fine-grained yellowish marble. Restored parts: Upper part of head, brows, nose, lips, chin, eyes, neck; right arm from below middle of upper arm and entire club; left hand with apples; right hip and buttock; right leg, left ankle, part of skin and lower part of support. Breaks in left upper arm, skin. Plinth doubtful. Amelung said that the head does not belong to the body.

33. *Loc. cit.*

34. In this connection, note a marble statue of the Roman period in the Palazzo Pitti (*Einzelaufnahmen*, No. 231) which may possibly echo the Herakleia type once its restorations are subtracted, although the considerably greater width of the stance produces a rangier, springier effect.

35. *Einzelaufnahmen*, No. 2734. Restored parts: nose, left hand with apples, right forearm with club, right leg below middle of thigh, left foot, and lower part of support.

36. F. Studniczka, "Ausgrabungen in Carnuntum," *Archäologisch-epigraphische Mitteilungen aus Oesterreich-Ungarn*, VIII, 1884, pp. 73–74. Ht: 70 cm., including plinth. Coarse white marble with yellow patina. Head missing; left hand and wrist made separately. Club encircled at top by two metal rings. Plinth broken. Also cited and reproduced by A. von Domaszewski, "Die Religion des römischen Heeres," *Westdeutsche Zeitschrift für Geschichte und Kunst*, XIV, 1895, p. 49.

37. Aelius Lampridius, *Commodus Antoninus*, VIII, 5, 9; IX, 2, 6 (*Scriptores historiae augustae*, ed. by David Magie, *The Loeb Classical Library*, New York, 1922, I, pp. 284 ff.).

38. The popularity of this type is interestingly indicated by its appearance on two reliefs. One of them, the so-called Medea and Jason relief in the Museo Torlonia from the villa of the Quintilii (C. L. Visconti, *Les monuments de sculpture antique du Musée Torlonia*, Rome, 1884, No. 459, pp. 341–343, pl. CXVIII; Greek marble; length: 94 cm.; ht: 1.02 m.), quotes the type very closely in details such as the suggestion of the missing bow by means of the lightly touching fingers of the upright hand, in the lithe energy of the fourth-century type, and even in certain details of the hair and face reminiscent of the Syracuse statuette. The other relief, so far as it is preserved equally exact in its reproduction of the type, is a dedication to Mithras which employs a common Herakles type. From Dieburg. Ht: 44 cm.; width: 28 cm.; th: 9 cm. (Emile Espérandieu, *Recueil général des bas-reliefs, statues et bustes de la Gaule romaine*, Paris and Brussels, sup. XI, 1931, p. 167, No. 246).

A badly-worn coin of Herakleia in the De Luynes collection (Jean Babelon, *Catalogue de la collection de Luynes*, Paris, 1924, I, pl. XV, No. 429) may either reflect a related but somewhat different statuary type or constitute a numismatic variant of the stater discussed above.

Note the existence of a related type (however, lacking the lion's skin) on the imperial coinage of Herakleia Salbace (B. V. Head,

Obviously, this group of statues, of which the provenance is unknown, is primarily of interest in reflecting the iconographic type and the importance of the Herakleia archetype. These sculptures throw far less light on the stylistic characteristics of the archetype than do the statuettes previously considered.

Thus it seems clear that the Herakleia stater is not primarily a numismatic type, but the reproduction of a lost statue of local workmanship. The fame of this statue of Herakles is amply attested by the extensive degree to which it was reproduced in both statues and statuettes. These

Catalogue of the Greek Coins of Caria, Cos, Rhodes, etc. [Catalogue of the Greek Coins in the British Museum, IX], London, 1897, pl. XX, 8). Here, the reproduction of a base clearly indicates a statuary prototype. The Roman cult statue reproduced on this coin may have been dependent upon the Herakleia type.

reproductions, ranging from contemporary copies to Roman transformations, are alike in their common repetition of a basic iconographic and stylistic type. The relationship between the coin type and this statuary group is so defined that it not only insures their dependence upon a common archetype but, in addition, it affords a detailed picture of the type and style of the original. Furthermore, the fact that, with the exception of the figure from Carnuntum and the less significant Roman copies, every statuette of which the provenance is known is Italian, provides an interesting check on their South Italian workmanship. For, on the basis of their strict iconographic relationship to an otherwise unknown figure type, all the statues and statuettes discussed in this connection may be looked upon as documents of South Italian sculpture.

EPILOGUE

A NUMISMATIC approach to the sculpture of Southern Italy and Sicily in the classical period has made it possible to reconstruct a series of lost statues once visible in certain cities and sanctuaries of that region and to attribute a group of statues and statuettes to local ateliers of Magna Graecia and Sicily. If these attributions prove acceptable, the statues and statuettes should be compared with other local products, especially architectural sculptures and terracottas, and analyzed to determine whether they afford stylistic common denominators indicative of a provincial regional style or of specific artistic centres characteristic of that vital colonial world. Such an analysis lies beyond the scope of the present investigation. Yet, until it has been made, the material assembled here will not have been fully explored nor will it have yielded its general implications in regard to the style or styles of the region.

A numismatic approach to the sculpture of a given region must always remain supplementary to the more orthodox means of access. Nevertheless, it could, and should, be applied to the study of region after region of the classical world. For there can be little question that among the coin types of the fifth and fourth centuries, as well as of the Hellenistic and Roman periods, many a faithful reproduction of ancient sculpture is to be found.

1

2

3

4

5

6

7

FIG. 1. Galaria: obol

FIGS. 2–4. Metapontum: staters

FIGS. 5–7. Terina: staters

FIG. 8. Tarentum: stater

FIG. 9. Eryx: tetradrachm

FIG. 10. Metapontum: bronze

8

9

FIG. 11. Herakleia: diobol

FIG. 12. Herakleia: gold quarter-
stater

FIG. 13. Messana: tetradrachm

FIG. 14. Pandosia: stater

10

11

12

13

14

Figs. 1–8, 10–14, Reverse Types;
Fig. 9, Obverse

PLATE XV

APPENDIX

The following coins illustrated on Plate xv present types that in all probability stand in the same relationship to a statuary archetype as those discussed in the preceding pages. At the present time, however, I know of no analogous statues or statuettes which may be associated with them. In spite of this lack of monumental evidence, it may be useful to list these types in the hope that the investigations of other scholars or the finding of new material may yield the necessary missing evidence.

1. GALARIA, obol or litra, *ca.* 460 B.C.
Rev: ΓΑΛΑ. Dionysos standing toward left wearing chiton; kantharos in extended right hand, grapes in left.
Gardner, *The Types of Greek Coins,* pl. II, 2. Dated according to Head, *H.N.,* p. 139.

2. METAPONTUM, stater, *ca.* 470 B. C.
Rev: ΑΨΕΛΟΣΟ. ΑΕΘΛΟΝ (retrograde). Acheloos in human form, bearded, with bull's horns and ears, standing facing with chlamys draped loosely over arms, patera in outstretched right arm, reed in left.
Noe, *The Coinage of Metapontum, Part II,* pl. XXIV, 311.

3. METAPONTUM, stater, *ca.* 470 B.C.
Rev: Herakles standing toward left wearing lion's skin over head, its paws knotted over his chest, the remainder of the pelt hanging behind him. Holds patera over altar in outstretched right hand, club in left.[1]
Noe, *op. cit.,* pl. XXIV, 312.

4. METAPONTUM, stater, *ca.* 470 B.C.
Rev: Nude Herakles standing facing, head turned toward left. Right hand holds club over shoulder, left rests on hip.
Noe, *op. cit.,* pl. XXIV, 313.

5. TERINA, stater, *ca.* 480–450 B.C.
Rev: Winged female figure in chiton standing facing, head turned toward left, with branch arched over head and held in both raised hands. Kurt Regling, *Terina (66. Programm zum Winckelmannsfeste),* Berlin, 1906, pl. II, γ.

6. TERINA, stater, *ca.* 420–400 B. C.
Rev: Winged female figure standing facing left wearing chiton and himation. Holds kerykeion in right hand; right arm rests on right thigh, right leg raised on supposed rock (astragal?). Left arm rests on back.
Ibid., pl. II, θθ.

7. TERINA, stater, *ca.* 420–400 B.C.
Rev: Winged female figure standing toward left wearing chiton, leaning left elbow on column; holds kerykeion in outstretched right hand. In left field: bird on cippus.
Ibid., pl. II, ii.

8. TARENTUM, stater, *ca.* 473–466 B.C.
Rev: Male figure wearing himation with end thrown over left shoulder seated toward right on four-legged stool over which panther's skin. Holds kantharos in extended right hand, distaff in left.
Grose, pl. XXI, 17.

9. ERYX, tetradrachm, *ca.* 431–371 B.C.
Obv: ΕΡΥΚΙΝΟΝ Aphrodite seated toward left wearing chiton and himation, with dove perched on hand; Eros stands before her.
Gardner, *op. cit.,* pl. VI, 3. Dated 413–400 B.C. by Head, *H.N.,* p. 138.

10. METAPONTUM, bronze, 350–300 B.C.
Rev: ΜΕΤΑ "Persephone" standing facing, head toward left, wearing long chiton and wreath of barley; left hand on hip, right holding long torch with crosspieces.
Grose, pl. XXXV, 24.

1. A fragmentary statue of Herakles in the Vatican, Galleria lapidaria no. 132 (Walter Amelung, *Die Sculpturen des Vaticanischen Museums,* Berlin, I, 1903, p. 261, pl. XXVII), which at first sight offers marked analogies to the Metapontine stater is actually not to be confused with this coin type since it must be restored with a club leaning against the left shoulder and held in the left arm about which the lion's skin is wrapped.

The resulting statuary type is similar, in this respect, to a bronze statuette illustrated by Max Silber, "Die Herkules-Statuette von der Grossglocknerstrasse," *J.O.A.I.,* XXXI, 1938–1939, Beiblatt, col. 5.

11. HERAKLEIA, diobol, *ca.* 380–281 B.C.
Rev: Herakles standing slightly toward right, weight on his left leg, right to side, with lion's skin over left arm and bow in left hand; right hand grasps club which leans against thigh. EY in left field; Nike flying to right to crown Herakles.
Grose, pl. XXIX, 4.

12. HERAKLEIA, gold quarter-stater, *ca.* 370–281 B.C.
Rev: Youthful Herakles seated to right on rock. Right arm rests on right knee and supports chin; left rests on club. ΦΙΛ in right field.
Babelon, *Catalogue de la collection de Luynes,* I, pl. XV, 420.[2]

2. *Ca.* 400 B.C., Pandosia issued a type representing a male figure seated toward left, his left hand leaning on the rocky seat, his outstretched right hand holding a patera (Mirone, "Copies de statues . . . de la Grande Grèce," *R.N.,* ser. IV, vol. XXVIII, 1925, pl. I, no. 20). Very likely, it should be added to this list. Note, however, the similar type struck by Mesma, *ca.* 350 B.C. (*idem.,* "Les divinités fluviales sur les monnaies antiques de la Grande Grèce," *R.N.,* ser. IV, vol. XXXI, 1928, p. 2 and pl. I, no. 3). Whether both coin types reflect a common statuary archetype or the Mesma variety depends upon a local statue in turn related to one in nearby Pandosia cannot be said. Whatever their interrelationships, a statuary archetype is very possibly at the root of this type.
About the middle of the fifth century B.C., a draped female

The following numbers are sufficiently related to statuary types discussed in this volume to warrant their tentative inclusion in this list. In both cases, however, it is quite possible that the numismatic type is loosely dependent upon painting or relief rather than upon sculpture in the round.

13. MESSANA, tetradrachm, *ca.* 461–396 B.C.
Rev: ΠΑΝ Nude, youthful Pan seated toward left on rock covered with nebris, holding lagobolon in left hand, caressing hare before him with right.
Imhoof-Blumer, *Monnaies grecques,* pl. B.5.

14. PANDOSIA, stater, *ca.* 400 B.C.
Rev: ΠΑΝΔΟΣΙΝ Youthful hunter seated on rocks looking back toward right. Leans on rocks with left hand, holds spear in right. Beside him, dog; in front, herm with kerykeion affixed.
Fig. 14 from Regling, *op. cit.,* pl. III, 9. Dated according to Head, *H.N.,* p. 106.

figure standing before an altar appeared on the coinage of several Sicilian cities — Enna, Entella, Eryx, and Himera. Although one or another of these figures may reflect a statue, they are so interrelated that it seems wiser, for the moment, to look upon them as numismatic variants of an artistic type.

ADDENDUM

As this volume goes to press, Antonio García y Bellido, *Los hallazgos griegos de España,* Madrid, 1936, has become available after long delay. For documentation of the discovery and early history of the bronze statuette discussed above on p. 28 before it passed into the collection of the Metropolitan Museum of Art and for additional bibliography see No. 19, pp. 66 ff. and pls. XXXVII–XL. The fact that the statuette was found on Mallorca is of particular interest in that it reinforces the present South Italian attribution given the proximity of the two regions.

GENERAL INDEX

INDEX OF MUSEUMS AND COLLECTIONS
containing statues and statuettes discussed in this volume